Acknowledgments

It has been a delight to work with the staff members at C&T Publishing—Roxane, Gailen, Amy, Liz, Kathryn, Linda, Alice, Tim, and Estefany, among others. Without their help of expertise and knowledge, I could never have written this book.

Another thanks to the generosity of fabric, thread, and batting companies: Maywood Studios, Robert Kauffman Fabrics, Aurifil, and Hobbs Batting.

CONTENTS

BARBARA H. CLINE

Diamond Star Quilts

Easy Construction ◆ 12 Skill-Building Projects

C&T PUBLISHING

Text copyright © 2020 by Barbara H. Cline

Photography and artwork copyright © 2020 by C&T Publishing, Inc.

Publisher: Amy Barrett-Daffin

Creative Director: Gailen Runge

Acquisitions Editor: Roxane Cerda

Managing Editor: Liz Aneloski

Editor: Kathryn Patterson

Technical Editor: Linda Johnson

Cover/Book Designer: April Mostek

Production Coordinator: Tim Manibusan

Production Editor: Alice Mace Nakanishi

Illustrators: Valyrie Gillum and Linda Johnson

Photo Assistants: Gregory Ligman and Lauren Herberg

Photography by Estefany Gonzalez of C&T Publishing, Inc.,
unless otherwise noted

Published by C&T Publishing, Inc., P.O. Box 1456, Lafayette, CA 94549

Library of Congress Control Number: 2020935647

Printed in China

10 9 8 7 6 5 4 3 2 1

INTRODUCTION

Eight-Pointed Stars Made from Diamonds

This is a teaching guide to sewing eight-pointed stars made from diamonds. The book starts with basic star patterns and as you move along you will learn more creative steps in making more complex stars. In the first four-star sampler project, you will learn how to piece a 12″ Eight-Pointed Star block. Next, you will make a 10″ Star block from diamonds cut from a strip set, using a diamond ruler or a template. After that, you will learn how to cut and sew strip sets together to make a lone star; and, for the last star in this project, you will learn to piece small diamonds with larger diamonds. As you work through the book, the progression of quilts will also be skill building. There will be quilts pieced with smaller patches, quilts that have pieced diamond blocks, and quilts with design elements outside of the star layout.

Let's look at how an eight-pointed star made from diamonds is different from an eight-pointed star made from half-square triangles. Notice in the diagram how the star is made up of equilateral diamonds, meaning all sides of each diamond measure the same length. The star made with half-square triangle squares is made up of "diamonds" with two shorter sides and two longer sides, plus there is a seam in the middle of each "diamond." This makes the diamond look lopsided, where the equilateral diamond does not have the lopsided effect.

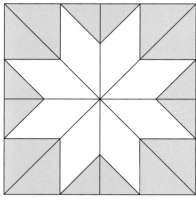
Created with equilateral diamonds

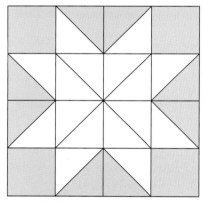
Created with half-square triangles

Think of an eight-pointed star as being a layout of a quilt. By cutting the large diamond in the eight-pointed star into smaller diamonds you come up with smaller diamond blocks inside a large diamond block. Each star in the book is identified as having different size diamond layouts. Here are two examples.

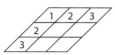

3 × 3 diamond layout

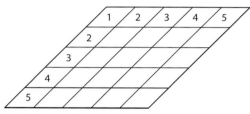

5 × 5 diamond layout

This means the diamonds are all 45° diamonds and there are diamonds inside of the large diamonds. Just like a square block layout can be made of many smaller squares, so an eight-pointed star layout is made of many diamonds. Notice in *Sampler Project* (page 17) that block 3 is a 4 × 4 diamond layout and the diamonds make a radiant starburst design by changing the colors. This is known as a *traditional lone star layout*.

The quilt designs in this book are made with a combination of whole diamonds and slant diamonds or reversed slant diamonds. The different star designs are created by using these three different diamond blocks.

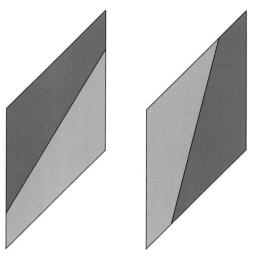

Slant diamond and reversed slant diamond

Here is a great option if you are interested in making a bigger quilt from one of the smaller quilt patterns in this book. Most of the quilts in this book measure 48″ × 48″. If you want to make a larger quilt, my first book, *Star Struck Quilts*, has a chapter on how to turn a 48″ × 48″ quilt into a twin- or queen-size quilt.

DIAMOND QUILT BASICS

Seams that measure an accurate ¼″ are very important in piecing eight-pointed stars. Here is one way to check your accuracy:

1. Cut 6 strips 1½″ × 5″ from a fabric.

2. Sew these strips together and press the seams in one direction.

3. Measure the width of the strip set; it should measure 6½″.

4. If the set measures more than 6½″, then you need to make the seam allowances larger.

5. If it measures less than 6½″, you need to make the seam allowances smaller.

When measuring a ¼″ sewing line with a ruler, the ¼″ line needs to be on the thread line and the edge of the ruler flush with the fabric edge.

TIP Pressing

When seams are pressed in one direction, they make a slightly bigger seam than when pressed open. This is why a scant ¼″ is used when piecing strip sets. A *scant* is only a thread width.

SUPPLIES NEEDED

- Rotary cutter, with a sharp new blade
- Rotary cutting mat, 24″ × 36″
- Rotary cutting rulers, 6″ × 24″ and 4″ × 14″ (The smaller ruler is best for cutting smaller pieces from strips and strip sets.)
- 45° diamond ruler 2½″ or larger (optional)
- Template plastic (if you are not using a 45° diamond ruler)
- Pins
- Sewing thread to match fabric
- ¼″-wide presser foot
- Scissors for clipping threads and trimming dog-ears
- Seam ripper
- Double-sided clear adhesive tape
- Sandpaper dots
- Fabric marking pencil
- Light spray starch (helps prevent fabric from getting distorted when working with diamonds that are cut on the bias)

Supplies for Bonus Project: Wedding Star (page 90)
- Template plastic
- Double-sided fusible web (My preference is Steam-A-Seam 2.)
- 1 spool of variegated thread
- Walking foot

Cutting from Templates

MAKING PLASTIC TEMPLATES FOR THE PROJECTS

1. Make a photocopy of the pattern(s) needed (pages 93–95).

2. Roughly cut out the shapes, leaving at least a ¼″ margin around each shape.

3. Attach the photocopy to the template plastic with double-sided clear adhesive tape. Apply the tape on the right side of the paper. Then place the template plastic on top of the paper (you can see through the plastic) and cut out each template shape, just cutting off the line. Leave the paper on the template plastic so there is no need to mark the letter or grainlines on the template plastic.

> ### TIP Making Your Templates Nonslip
>
> Add a few sandpaper dots or a few pieces of double-sided tape to the paper on the underside of each template. This helps keep the templates from sliding on the fabric when you are cutting around them.

CUTTING THE PIECES

Using the templates to cut the pieces from fabric strips is the easiest and most efficient cutting method. It eliminates making little cuts in the fabric and requires fewer rotations of the template.

Never cut folded fabric except where noted. The right side of the fabric always needs to be facing up. When cutting shapes from a fabric strip, rotate or slide the template into the next position; never flip the template over unless the instructions specifically tell you to flip it.

CUTTING THE D SHAPES

1. Cut a strip 3¾″ × width of fabric (WOF).

2. Place the fabric strip right side up on the cutting mat and place the template on the fabric strip near one end.

3. Place the ruler on top of the template, aligning the ¼″ line of the ruler to the ¼″ line on the template, and cut with a rotary cutter. Using this method, you will never need to worry about shaving off the template plastic.

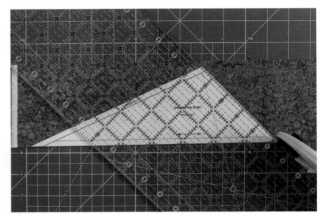

Place grainline parallel to edge of cut strips.

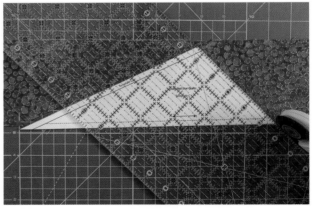

Rotate template and continue cutting.

Cutting Diamonds

1. For all the diamonds in this book, your cuts will be at a 45° angle. To achieve this angle, place the strip parallel to the bottom edge of the cutting mat, lining up the edge on a horizontal grid line. Place the ruler on top of the fabric, aligning the ruler's 45° line with the horizontal edge of the cut strip. Cut on this angle. This initial cut will create the first edge of the diamond.

2. Refer to the instructions for the desired diamond width. Use a ruler to measure the width from the first cut edge, keeping the ruler at the same 45° angle. Make the next cut. Repeat along the length of the strip to make the number of cuts required for the project.

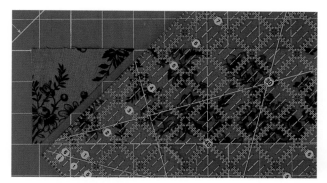

45° angle cut on single strip

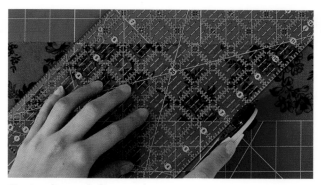

Cutting diamonds from single strip

CUTTING LONG DIAMONDS

When you are rotary cutting single diamonds and diamond strips that are not equilateral, you will cut either to the upper right or to the upper left, depending on the project instructions. Each cutting direction produces a unique diamond, and it is important to keep the terms distinct: Diagonal cuts to the right produce right long diamonds; diagonal cuts to the left produce left long diamonds. The illustration shows the two types of long diamonds. In all long diamond subcutting, the right side of the fabric must always be facing up. If you wish, you can stack the strips and cut double fabric layers, but never fold these strips.

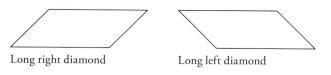

Long right diamond   Long left diamond

Cutting Strip Sets

> **TIP**
>
> When sewing strip sets together, always sew the next seam in the opposite direction. This helps prevent making a curved strip set.

CREATING A STRIP SET

In some projects, you will create strip sets to speed up the diamond cutting process. Specific information about the numbers of strips and their widths will be given in the project instructions. Here are some strip set basics for your reference.

* Always place the fabric faceup to cut on the mat.

* As you arrange the strip set, offset the strips by the width of the strip.

- The order and direction in which you arrange and sew the strips will determine the pattern.

- Before cutting, orient the strip sets as shown in the diagrams to achieve the correct cuts. Having strips upside down can produce "misfit" strips.

- All the diamonds and diamond strips in this book are cut at a 45° angle.

The following is just an example of a strip set. A particular project may have you arranging the strips as stair steps in the opposite direction. Each project will have specific instructions and illustrations for the strip sets and the direction of the cuts.

1. Place strip 1 on your cutting mat, right side up.

2. Place strip 2 beneath strip 1. Offset the left edge of this strip by the width of the strip as shown. Repeat for strips 3–5.

| Strip 1 |
| Strip 2 |
| Strip 3 |
| Strip 4 |
| Strip 5 |

3. Pin and sew the strips together in their proper order. To keep the strips from curving, sew the seams in alternating directions, and let the sewing machine do the work. Do not pull on the fabric strips as you sew. Press the seams in the direction indicated in the project instructions.

ROTARY CUTTING DIAMOND STRIPS AND SEWING ROWS TOGETHER

1. For all the diamond strips in this book, your cuts will be at a 45° angle. To achieve this angle, place the strip or strip set parallel to the bottom edge of the cutting mat, lining up the edge on a horizontal grid line. Place the ruler on top of the fabric, aligning the ruler's 45° line with the horizontal edge of the cut strip. This initial cut will create the first edge of the diamond or diamond strip.

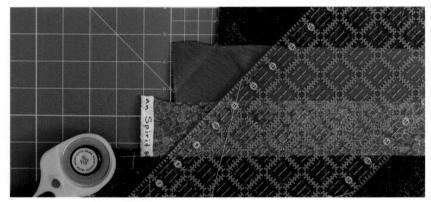

45° angle cut on strip set

2. Refer to the project instructions for the desired strip set width. Use a ruler to measure the width from the first cut edge, keeping the ruler at the same 45° angle. Make the next cut. Repeat along the length of the strip set to make the number of cuts required for the project.

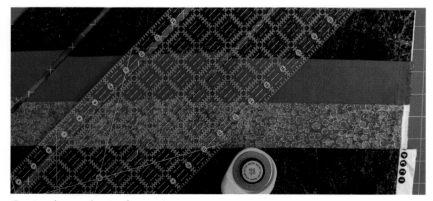

Cutting diamond strips from strip sets

3. To join 2 diamond strips, place strips right sides together. Align each seam of the strip, and secure with pins. Then sew the seam. Check for seam alignment before pressing the seam.

Pinning diamond star strips

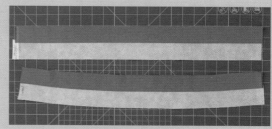

Straight and curved strip sets

Cutting Split Diamonds

The split diamonds are cut at a slant, which means the center seam does not hit the middle of the diamond tip. This keeps bulk to a minimum whenever they are used in the center of an eight-pointed star; since the seams are slanted, there will be 8 points coming together instead of 16 points.

If you prefer, substitute template plastic for the acrylic ruler. Either method will aid in cutting the split diamonds. (Refer to Making Plastic Templates for the Projects, page 10.)

1. Make a copy of the 2½˝ diamond B pattern (page 94) or the 2½˝ diamond Br (reverse) pattern (page 94). It is very important to use the correct diamond for each project. Cut the paper template out on its outer lines.

2. Place double-sided clear adhesive tape on the right side of the paper template. Then place the 45°, 2½", or larger acrylic diamond ruler on top of the paper template. Make sure the 2 edges of the paper are lined up with the 45° point of the ruler.

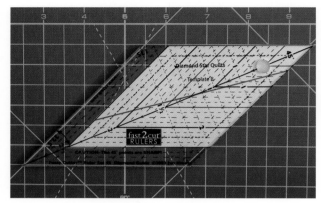

Paper template with acrylic ruler taped on top

3. Place the ruler on the pieced strip set and match the red line on the template with the seamline on the fabric strip. Cut on 2 sides of the template.

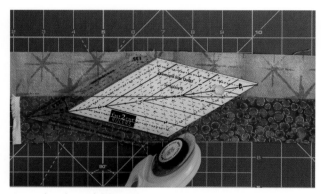

Cut right edges of diamond.

4. Rotate the ruler and cut the other 2 sides of the diamond.

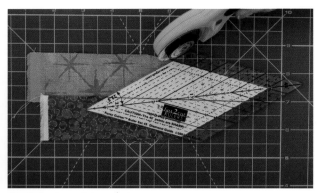

Cut left edges of diamond.

5. Continue down the strip to cut the split diamonds.

TIP Cutting Tip

Cut the side of the diamond on the right first, move the fabric strip away, and then cut the rest of the diamond. This makes it so there are no little cuts in the fabric strip where the next diamond will be cut.

Basic Piecing Order

The Diamond Star blocks in this book are composed of 8 diamonds that make up the points of the star, and 16 triangles—large and small—that make up the block background.

1. Lay out all the patches for an eight-pointed star. See how the large triangles form a square in each corner and the small triangles form a larger triangle in the middle of each side of the block. Triangles are *always* sewn to either side of the *outside tip* of the diamond.

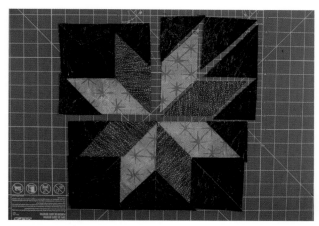

Lay out complete star.

2. Pin and sew 2 triangles—1 large and 1 small—to a diamond. Whenever the right sides of a diamond are sewn to the right side of a triangle, the sewing line will cross where the 2 fabrics intersect each other. Look at the sewing line in the photo and notice the stitching is where the 2 different fabrics intersect; I call this a *V*. When you sew the ¼″ seam your needle needs to be at the center of the V. This will take place when you start sewing and when you come to the end of the seam.

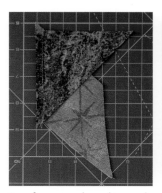
Sew first triangle to diamond.

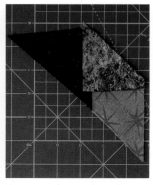
Sew second triangle to diamond.

TIP Triangle Units

Placement of the triangles does make a difference! When a small triangle is sewn to the left side of the diamond's outside tip, and a large triangle is sewn to the right, the result is an A triangle unit. When the large triangle is sewn to the left, and small triangle to the right, a B triangle unit is created. (See the diagram below.) Each Diamond Star requires 4 A and 4 B triangle units, each equals one-eighth of a star. Alternating A and B triangle units makes a standard square Diamond Star block.

3. Sew the A and B triangle unit into eighths and into fourths; make 4. Press in the same direction.

4. Sew the fourths into halves; make 2. Press in the same direction.

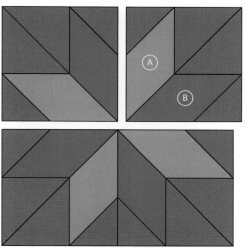

Sew according to exploded diagram
(1 A + 1 B triangle unit = ¼ block).

5. Sew the halves together. Press the center seam so the seams all flow in either the clockwise or counterclockwise direction.

6. Trim all the dog-ears with scissors or a rotary cutter.

TIP Sewing Tip

Option 1   Sometimes when sewing the point of a triangle or diamond, the tip will get distorted and the seam allowance will be small. This happens because the fabric is only catching on one side of the feed dogs. To keep this from happening try using a thread catcher, which is a small folded piece of fabric about ½″ wide and 1″ long. This is used at the beginning and at the end of each seam to help grasp the diamond or triangle points at the ¼″ seam allowance.

Option 2   A piece of paper can also be used to start sewing on. Place a small adhesive-backed paper note under the triangle or diamond tip with the sticky side against the fabric, and then sew. Tear away the paper.

Sewing Diamonds to Diamonds

When sewing two diamonds together, you will also have a V on both ends of the seam. The photo shows where your stitching line will fall. Always press the seam away from the center of the star.

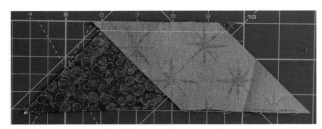

Sewing line hits the V

TIP How to Match Center Points

When sewing two quarters together, the points must match correctly. If they do not match at this point, they will never match when the eight-pointed star is complete.

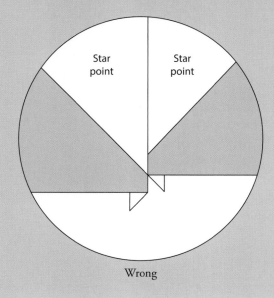

Wrong

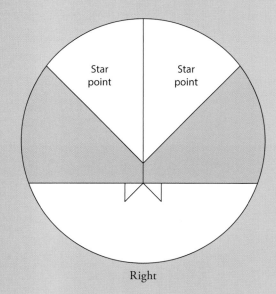

Right

Sampler Project

FINISHED QUILT: 53″ × 53″

From this project, you will learn how to piece four versions of the basic eight-pointed star. The techniques you will learn are how to cut diamonds from a strip, how to strip piece, and how to cut and work with smaller diamond pieces.

MATERIALS

Yardage is based on 42"-wide fabric.

Dark red: ⅜ yard

Bright red: ⅝ yard

Orange: ⅜ yard

Light orange: ⅓ yard

Brown: 3½ yards

Binding: ½ yard

Backing: 61" × 61"

Batting: 61" × 61"

CUTTING

WOF is width of fabric. • *Block measurements are finished sizes.*
Refer to Cutting Diamonds (page 11) for more information about creating diamond shapes.

Block 1 (12" × 12")

Label all pieces Block 1.

Bright red

- Cut 1 strip 3" × WOF; subcut
  4 diamonds 3" wide.

Orange

- Cut 1 strip 3" × WOF; subcut
  4 diamonds 3" wide.

Brown

- Cut 1 strip 4⅜" × WOF; subcut:
  4 squares 4⅜" × 4⅜" and cut
  diagonally once for a total of
  8 large triangles
  4 squares 3⅜" × 3⅜" and cut
  diagonally once for a total of
  8 small triangles

Block 2 (10" × 10")

Label all pieces Block 2.

Light orange

- Cut 1 strip 1¾" × WOF.

Orange

- Cut 1 strip 1¾" × WOF.

Brown

- Cut 1 strip 3¾" × WOF; subcut:
  4 squares 3¾" × 3¾" and cut
  diagonally once for a total of
  8 large triangles
  4 squares 3" × 3" and cut
  diagonally once for a total of
  8 small triangles

Block 3 (38" × 38")

Label all pieces Block 3.

Dark red

- Cut 3 strips 2½" × WOF.

Bright red

- Cut 4 strips 2½" × WOF.

Orange

- Cut 2 strips 2½" × WOF.

Light orange

- Cut 1 strip 2½" × WOF.

Brown

- Cut 2 strips 12" × WOF; subcut
  4 squares 12" × 12" and cut
  diagonally once for a total of
  8 large triangles.
- Cut 1 strip 8¾" × WOF; subcut
  4 squares 8¾" × 8¾" and cut
  diagonally once for a total of
  8 small triangles.
- Cut 6 strips 2½" × WOF.

Block 4 (18" × 18")

Label all pieces Block 4.

Dark red

- Cut 1 strip 1¾" × WOF.

Bright red

- Cut 2 strips 1¾" × WOF.

Light orange

- Cut 2 strips 1¾" × WOF.

Brown

- Cut 1 strip 6⅛" × WOF; subcut
  4 squares 6⅛" × 6⅛" and cut
  diagonally once for a total of
  8 large triangles.
- Cut 1 strip 4⅝" × WOF; subcut
  4 squares 4⅝" × 4⅝" and cut
  diagonally once for a total of
  8 small triangles.
- Cut 1 strip 3" × WOF; subcut
  8 diamonds at a 45° angle.

Cutting continued →

Background

Brown

- Cut 1 strip 13½″ × WOF; subcut:

  1 rectangle 13½″ × 9½″
  (Section 1, C)

  1 rectangle 12½″ × 13½″
  (Section 3, B)

  1 rectangle 11½″ × 12½″
  (Section 4, B)

- Cut 1 strip 7½″ × WOF;
  subcut 1 rectangle 7½″ × 12½″
  (Section 2, B).

- Cut 1 strip 3½″ × WOF; subcut
  1 strip 3½″ × 10½″ (Section 1, B).

- Cut 3 strips 2½″ × WOF. Sew ends
  together and subcut:

  1 strip 2½″ × 53½″ (Border C)

  1 strip 2½″ × 51½″ (Border B)

- Cut 2 strips 2½″ × WOF; subcut:

  1 strip 2½″ × 32½″ (Border A)

  1 strip 2½″ × 18½″ (Section 3, D)

- Cut 1 strip 1½″ × WOF; subcut
  1 strip 1½″ × 19½″ (Section 2, C).

Binding

- Cut 6 strips 2¼″ × WOF.

Making the Blocks

This project is designed for learning different techniques in piecing eight-pointed stars. The first Star block is a basic eight-pointed star, the second Star block has split diamonds made from a strip set, the third Star block is made from strip sets, and the fourth Star block is made by strip piecing, then joining units to basic diamonds to make larger diamonds.

BLOCK 1: BASIC EIGHT-POINTED STAR

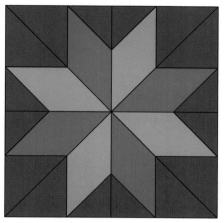

12″ finished block

Arrange all the pieces labeled Block 1 to make a Star block. Following the instructions in Basic Piecing Order (page 15), sew the block together in the order shown.

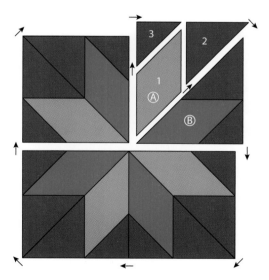

BLOCK 2: SPLIT-DIAMOND STAR

Block 2 is made by piecing 2 strips of fabric together and then using a template to cut a split diamond. The offset red line of the template aligns with the seam of the strip set. Notice how the seam of the diamond will not end up in the diamond's tips. By making the diamonds with this technique, there are still 8 points in the center of the star instead of 16 points.

1. Following the instructions for Creating a Strip Set (page 11), sew light orange and orange strips together. Press the seams toward the darker fabric.

2. Make a template from the 3½" diamond A pattern (page 93). (Refer to Cutting from Templates, page 10, for more information about making and using templates.)

3. Following the instructions for Cutting Split Diamonds (page 13), place template A on top of the strip set, matching the red centerline of the template with the seamline. Cut 8 diamonds.

Line up red line on template with seamline.

4. Arrange the triangles and split diamonds as shown. Following the instructions in Basic Piecing Order (page 15), sew the block together in the order shown.

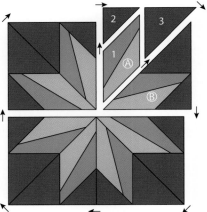

Sewing order

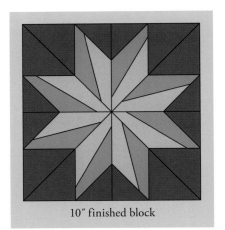

10" finished block

BLOCK 3: STRIP-SET DIAMOND STAR

The technique used in this block is strip piecing. You will make 4 different strip sets, cut the sets into diamond strips, and sew the strips together. (Refer to Cutting Strip Sets, page 11, for more detailed information about piecing, cutting, and sewing rows of strips to make a diamond.)

1. Following the instructions for Creating a Strip Set (page 11), sew the strips together as shown. The strip sets should measure 8½″ wide. Press in the direction of the arrows.

2. Trim the left edge of the set at a 45° angle. Cut 8 diamond strips 2½″ wide from each strip set.

38″ finished block

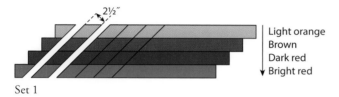

2½″

Light orange
Brown
Dark red
Bright red

Set 1

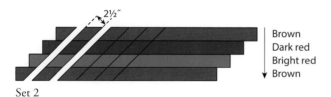

2½″

Brown
Dark red
Bright red
Brown

Set 2

2½″

Dark red
Bright red
Brown
Orange

Set 3

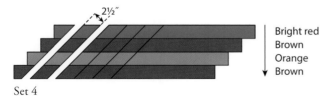

2½″

Bright red
Brown
Orange
Brown

Set 4

3. Arrange the diamond strips as shown to make a diamond. Place the strips in order; then pin and sew together. (Refer to Rotary Cutting Diamond Strips and Sewing Rows Together, page 12.)

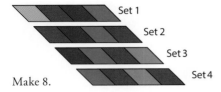

Set 1
Set 2
Set 3
Set 4

Make 8.

4. Add the large and small triangles to the diamonds to make 4 A and 4 B triangle units.

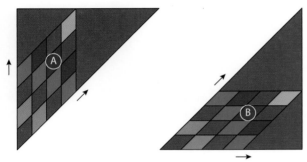

Make 4 A triangle units.　　　Make 4 B triangle units.

5. Sew A and B triangle units together, pinning and matching all the seams. Make 3.

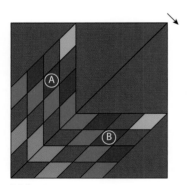

Make 3.

6. Do *not* join the fourth pair of A and B triangle units. Instead, cut a 6¾″ × 6¾″ square of paper, and then cut once diagonally. Use the paper triangle to trim the large brown triangles as shown. (This is only for the fourth pair of A and B triangle units.)

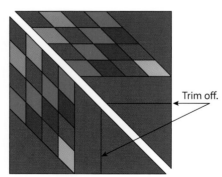

Trim off.

Make 2 cuts.

BLOCK 4: STRIP-PIECED AND BASIC DIAMOND STAR

1. Following the instructions for Cutting Diamonds (page 11), cut 8 diamonds 3″ wide from the brown 3″ strip at a 45° angle.

2. Following the instructions for Creating a Strip Set (page 11), sew dark red, bright red, and light orange 1¾″ strips together to make a strip set.

3. Keeping the light orange on top, cut 8 strips 1¾″ wide at a 45° angle to the right. (Refer to Rotary Cutting Diamond Strips and Sewing Rows Together, page 12.)

Light orange
Bright red
Dark red

Cut slant to the right.

4. Sew the bright red and light orange 1¾″ strips together to make a strip set.

5. Keeping the light orange on top, cut 8 strips 1¾″ wide at a 45° angle to the left. (Refer to Cutting Strip Sets, page 11.)

Bright red
Light orange

Cut slant to the left.

6. Following the instructions for Sewing Diamonds to Diamonds (page 16), sew the bright red / light orange pair of diamonds to the large diamond.

7. Sew the strip set of 3 to the adjacent side of the unit.

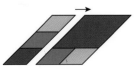

Make 8.

18″ finished block

8. Following the instructions in Basic Piecing Order (page 15), sew the large and small triangles onto the diamonds as shown to make 4 A triangle units and 4 B triangle units.

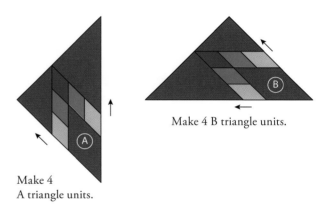

Make 4 B triangle units.

Make 4 A triangle units.

9. Sew A and B units together to make 2 triangular half-blocks. Do not sew these half-blocks together at this time. They will be sewn together when assembling the quilt.

Make 2 of each.

Assembling and Finishing the Quilt

1. Arrange all the pieces of the quilt and sew together by section, according to the quilt assembly diagram (below). Follow the alphabetical sequence within each section.

2. Once the 4 sections have been assembled, sew Sections 3 and 4 together.

3. Add Section 2 to the left side of Section 3/4 to make the bottom portion of the quilt.

4. Attach strip A to the right side of the bottom portion (Section 2/3/4).

5. Sew Section 1 to the top of the bottom portion. Attach Borders B and C in that order.

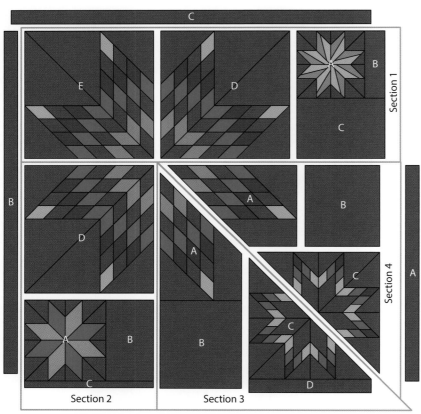

Quilt assembly

6. Use your favorite methods to layer, quilt, and bind the quilt with the binding strips. (Refer to Quiltmaking Basics: How to Finish Your Quilt, page 87, for more detailed information.)

Here is a great simple way to quilt *Sampler Project.* I used a walking foot and quilted a slight wave over the quilt, then echoed the quilting 4 times. On the next echo quilting, I went to the center of the quilt and then turned a 45° angle and quilted an arch. I then echo quilted this line 4 times. After that step, I again started to echo quilt but went to the center of the quilt,

turned about a 22° angle (I am roughly trying to quilt an arch between the last sections made), and then echo quilted this line 4 times. I continued on until the quilt was completely quilted.

Close-up of quilting

Quilting

QUILTS MADE FROM STRIP SETS

Echo Star

FINISHED QUILT: 48″ × 48″ ♦ 5 × 5 diamond layout

Echo Star is strip-pieced using 2½″-wide strips. I chose a precut 2½″ strip bundle and separated the dark and light values of fabrics. For the background, I used light fabrics that would contrast well with the dark 2½″ precut strips.

MATERIALS

Yardage is based on 42"-wide fabric.

Dark fabrics (8): ¼ yard *each*

Light fabrics (5): ¼ yard *each*

Light background fabrics (6):
½ yard *each*

Binding: ½ yard

Backing: 56" × 56"

Batting: 56" × 56"

CUTTING

WOF is width of fabric.

Dark fabrics (8)

◆ Cut 2 strips 2½" × WOF
  from *each* fabric.

Light fabrics (5)

◆ Cut 2 strips 2½" × WOF
  from *each* fabric.

Light background fabrics (6)

◆ Cut 1 strip 15" × WOF
  from *each* fabric; subcut:
  1 square 15" × 15" and cut
  diagonally once for a total
  of 2 large triangles
  1 square 11" × 11" and cut
  diagonally once for a total
  of 2 small triangles

Binding

◆ Cut 5 strips 2¼" × WOF.

Making the Pieced Diamonds

Refer to Cutting Strip Sets (page 11) for more detailed instructions about making, cutting, and sewing diamonds made from strip sets.

1. Sew the strips together as shown. The strip sets should measure 10½" wide. Press in the direction of the arrows.

Set 1 — Dark, Dark, Dark, Dark, Dark

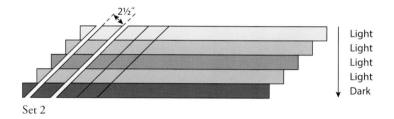

Set 2 — Light, Light, Light, Light, Dark

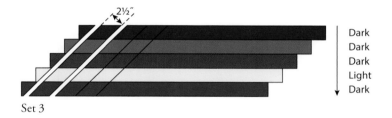

Set 3 — Dark, Dark, Dark, Light, Dark

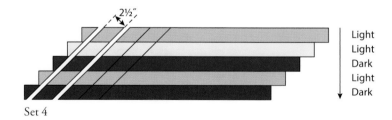

Set 4 — Light, Light, Dark, Light, Dark

Set 5 — Dark, Light, Dark, Light, Dark

2. Trim the left edge of the strip set at a 45° angle. Cut 8 diamond strips 2½″ wide from each strip set.

3. Arrange the diamond strips as shown to make a diamond. Place the strips in order; then pin and sew together. (Refer to Rotary Cutting Diamond Strips and Sewing Rows Together, page 12, for detailed instructions.)

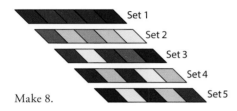

Make 8.

4. Following the instructions in Basic Piecing Order (page 15), sew the large and small triangles onto the diamonds as shown to make 4 A triangle units and 4 B triangle units.

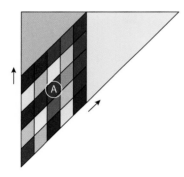

Make 4 A triangle units.

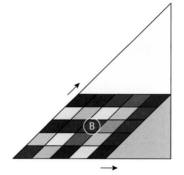

Make 4 B triangle units.

Assembling and Finishing the Quilt

1. Arrange all the pieces of the quilt and piece according to the quilt assembly diagram. (Refer to Basic Piecing Order, page 15.)

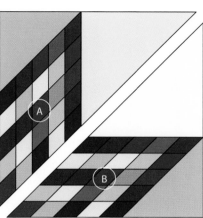

Quilt assembly

2. Use your favorite methods to layer, quilt, and bind the quilt with the binding strips. (Refer to Quiltmaking Basics: How to Finish Your Quilt, page 87, for more detailed instructions.)

Echo Star with Pinwheel

FINISHED QUILT: 48″ × 48″ ◆ 4 × 4 diamond layout

Strip piecing is the technique used in piecing this quilt. (If you have made *Sampler Project*, page 17, Block 3 also used strip piecing.) The added feature in this quilt is there is a pinwheel design outside of the eight-pointed star.

MATERIALS

Yardage is based on 42"-wide fabric.

Light green: 1 yard

Dark green: 1 yard

Gray: 2⅞ yards

Binding: ½ yard

Backing: 56" × 56"

Batting: 56" × 56"

CUTTING

WOF is width of fabric.

Light green

- Cut 2 strips 2¼" × WOF; cut in half.
- Cut 1 strip 5¾" × WOF; cut in half.
- Cut 1 strip 10¾" × WOF; subcut:
  2 squares 10¾" × 10¾" and cut diagonally once for a total of 4 large triangles
  2 squares 7¾" × 7¾" and cut diagonally once for a total of 4 small triangles

Dark green

- Cut 2 strips 2¼" × WOF and cut in half.
- Cut 1 strip 5¾" × WOF and cut in half.
- Cut 1 strip 10¾" × WOF; subcut:
  2 squares 10¾" × 10¾" and cut diagonally once for a total of 4 large triangles
  2 squares 7¾" × 7¾" and cut diagonally once for a total of 4 small triangles

Gray

- Cut 2 strips 25¼" × WOF; subcut:
  1 square 25¼" × 25¼" and cut diagonally twice for a total of 4 triangles
  4 rectangles 7⅜" × 24½" and cut the right side at a 45° angle to the right on all 4 rectangles

- Cut 1 strip 7½" × WOF.
- Cut 1 strip 4" × WOF and cut in half.
- Cut 4 strips 2¼" × WOF and cut in half.

Binding

- Cut 5 strips 2¼" × WOF.

Making the Diamond Units

Refer to Cutting Strip Sets (page 11), for more instructions.

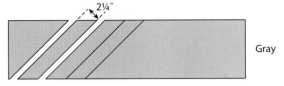

Set 1: Cut 8 strips.

Gray

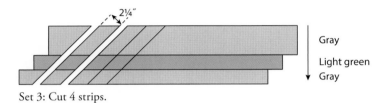

Light green

Gray

Set 2: Cut 4 strips.

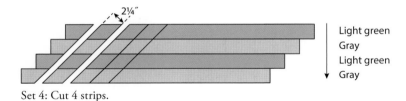

Gray

Light green

Gray

Set 3: Cut 4 strips.

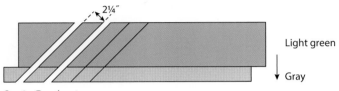

Light green

Gray

Light green

Gray

Set 4: Cut 4 strips.

Dark green

Gray

Set 5: Cut 4 strips.

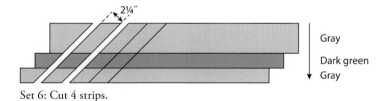

Gray

Dark green

Gray

Set 6: Cut 4 strips.

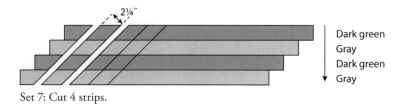

Dark green

Gray

Dark green

Gray

Set 7: Cut 4 strips.

1. Sew strips together as shown. The strip sets should measure 7½″ wide. Press in direction of arrows.

2. Trim the left edge of the strip sets at a 45° angle. Cut diamond strips 2¼″ wide from each strip set: 8 strips from strip set 1, 4 strips each from strip sets 2–7.

3. Arrange the diamond strips as shown to make a diamond. Place the strips in order; then pin and sew together. (Refer to Rotary Cutting Diamond Strips and Sewing Rows Together, page 12, for detailed instructions.)

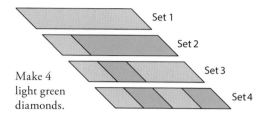

Make 4 light green diamonds.

Set 1
Set 2
Set 3
Set 4

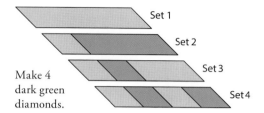

Make 4 dark green diamonds.

Set 1
Set 2
Set 3
Set 4

4. Arrange a large light green diamond with a large light green triangle and a small light green triangle. Sew together to make 4 A triangle units (Refer to Basic Piecing Order, page 15.) Add a trimmed gray strip.

5. Repeat Step 3 using diamonds and triangles in dark green. Sew together to make 4 A triangle units again, but this time add a large gray triangle.

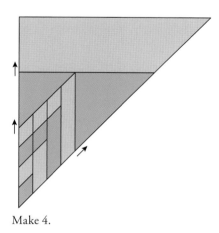

Make 4.

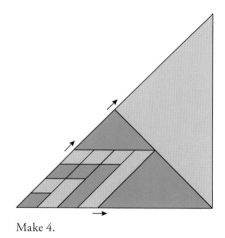

Make 4.

TIP Pinwheels from A Diamonds

Color placement, the absence of B triangle units, plus the irregular background shapes combine to create the giant pinwheel feature in this quilt.

Assembling and Finishing the Quilt

1. Arrange all the pieces of the quilt and piece according to the quilt assembly diagram. (Refer to Basic Piecing Order, page 15.)

Quilt assembly

2. Use your favorite methods to layer, quilt, and bind the quilt with the binding strips. (Refer to Quiltmaking Basics: How to Finish Your Quilt, page 87, for more detailed information.)

Twirling and A-Swirling

FINISHED QUILT: 48″ × 48″ ◆ 5 × 5 diamond layout

In the star strip set project *Echo Star* (page 28), all strips for the strip sets were cut the same size, 2½″ wide. In *Twirling and A-Swirling*, the strips are cut two different sizes, 2½″ and 1½″ wide. By placing the strip sets in different orders, a spinning star appears. Notice the background fabric in the star and how it creates floating elements that spin.

MATERIALS

Yardage is based on 42"-wide fabric.

Gray: ¾ yard

Purple: ⅝ yard

Navy: 2⅝ yards

Binding: ½ yard

Backing: 56" × 56"

Batting: 56" × 56"

CUTTING

WOF is width of fabric.

Gray

• Cut 14 strips 1½" × WOF.

Purple

• Cut 5 strips 2½" × WOF.

• Cut 2 strips 1½" × WOF.

Navy

• Cut 2 strips 15" × WOF; subcut:
  4 squares 15" × 15 and cut
  diagonally once for a total of
  8 large triangles

  1 square 11" × 11" and cut
  diagonally once for a total of
  2 small triangles

• Cut 1 strip 11" × WOF; subcut:
  3 squares 11" × 11" and cut
  diagonally once for a combined
  total of 8 small triangles.

• Cut 7 strips 2½" × WOF.

• Cut 10 strips 1½" × WOF.

Binding

• Cut 5 strips 2¼" × WOF.

Making the Diamond Units

Important: The strips are all cut at a left slant for this project.

1. Following the instructions for Creating a Strip Set (page 11), sew the strips together as shown. The strip sets should measure 10½" wide. Press in the direction of the arrows.

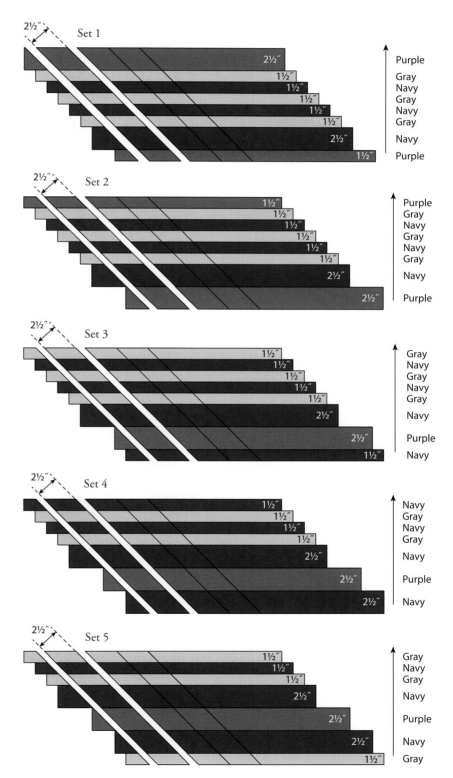

2. Trim the left edge of each set at a 45° angle to the left. Cut 8 diamond strips 2½″ wide from each strip set. (Refer to Rotary Cutting Diamond Strips and Sewing Rows Together, page 12, for detailed instructions.)

3. Arrange the diamond strips as shown to make a large diamond. Place the strips in order; then pin and sew together.

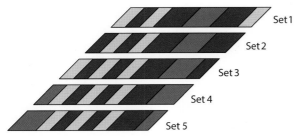

Make 8.

4. Add the large navy and small navy triangles to the large diamonds, making 4 A and 4 B triangle units. Sew an A and B triangle unit together making a quarter-square. (Refer to Basic Piecing Order, page 15, for more information.)

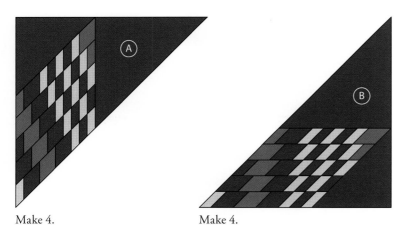

Make 4.   Make 4.

Assembling and Finishing the Quilt

1. Arrange all the quarter-squares of the quilt and piece together according to the quilt assembly diagram. (Refer to Basic Piecing Order, page 15.)

Quilt assembly

2. Use your favorite methods to layer, quilt, and bind the quilt with the binding strips. (Refer to Quiltmaking Basics: How to Finish Your Quilt, page 87, for more detailed information.)

QUILTS MADE WITH SPLIT DIAMONDS

The quilts in this chapter all have slant-pieced or split diamonds in the stars, which are cut from a strip set using a template. I have included a technique that makes cutting these diamonds easy by using paper templates (see Cutting Split Diamonds, page 13).

Cactus Star

FINISHED QUILT: 22″ × 22″ ♦ 3 × 3 diamond layout

If you have made *Sampler Project* (page 17), you have already made the split diamond.
The split diamond in *Cactus Star* is made with a finished 2″ diamond—and yet—
both the background piecing and trimming techniques are unique. The project is
small and fast and is great for a centerpiece on a table or as a small wall quilt.

MATERIALS

Yardage is based on 42"-wide fabric.

Dark red: ⅛ yard

Light red: ⅛ yard

Dark blue: ¼ yard

Light blue: ¼ yard

White tone-on-tone: 1 yard

Binding: ¼ yard

Backing: 30″ × 30″

Batting: 30″ × 30″

CUTTING

WOF is width of fabric.
Refer to Cutting Diamonds (page 11)
for more information about creating
diamond shapes.

Dark red

◆ Cut 1 strip 1¾″ × WOF.

Light red

◆ Cut 1 strip 1¾″ × WOF.

Dark blue

◆ Cut 2 strips 1¾″ × WOF.

Light blue

◆ Cut 2 strips 1¾″ × WOF.

White tone-on-tone

◆ Cut 4 strips 1¾″ × WOF.

◆ Cut 3 strips 2½″ × WOF;
  subcut 32 diamonds 2½″ wide.

◆ Cut 2 strips 7″ × WOF;
  subcut 8 squares 7″ × 7″ and
  cut diagonally once for a total
  of 16 triangles.

Binding

◆ Cut 3 strips 2¼″ × WOF.

Making the Split Diamonds

1. Following the instructions for Creating a Strip Set (page 11), sew the following strip sets. Press the seams toward the darker fabrics.

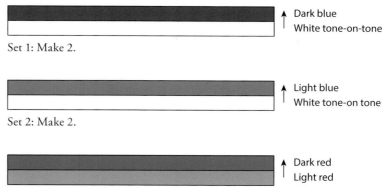

Set 1: Make 2.

Set 2: Make 2.

Set 3: Make 1.

2. Make templates from the 2½″ diamond B and 2½″ diamond Br patterns (page 94). (Refer to Cutting from Templates, page 10, for more information about making and using templates.)

3. Following the instructions for Cutting Split Diamonds (page 13), cut 8 split diamonds from each of the strip sets, using template B. Label B diamonds.

4. From each of strip sets 1 and 2, cut 8 split diamonds, using template Br (reverse). Label Br diamonds.

Making the Large Diamonds

Piece 8 large diamonds using white tone-on-tone diamonds and split diamonds as shown.

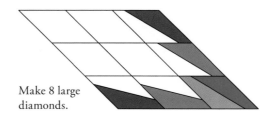

Make 8 large diamonds.

Assembling and Finishing the Quilt

In this instance, because much of the quilt block's background will be trimmed, the triangles between the diamonds are all the same size in order to save fabric. The final shape of the block *before* trimming will not be square, but rather octagonal.

1. Arrange the 8 large diamond sections with the 16 white tone-on-tone triangles. Sew the hypotenuse of the tone-on-tone triangles to each side of the outside diamond tips. All 8 diamonds will be identical.

2. Follow the quilt assembly diagram to assemble the star.

Quilt assembly

3. To trim the block to size, start at the outer tip of a diamond and draw a connecting line to the tip of every other diamond using an erasable marker. This marks the seamline. Cut ¼″ beyond the marked line to include seam allowance. The block now measures 22½″ × 22½″.

Trimming the block

4. Use your favorite methods to layer, quilt, and bind the quilt with the binding strips. (Refer to Quiltmaking Basics: How to Finish Your Quilt, page 87, for more detailed information.)

Large Quilt Option

Here is a quilt option using 12 different Cactus Star blocks.

Color option for a larger quilt (finished quilt: 66″ × 88″)

Spiky Desert Rose

FINISHED QUILT: 48″ × 48″ ♦ 3 × 3 diamond layout

This quilt resembles *Cactus Star* (page 44) but uses larger diamonds and features outer "spikes." Unlike *Cactus Star*, the block is not trimmed down, and it also has borders around it.

MATERIALS

Yardage is based on 42"-wide fabric.

Dark red: ⅝ yard

Light red: ¼ yard

Dark green: ½ yard

Light green: ½ yard

Black: 3 yards

Binding: ½ yard

Backing: 57" × 57"

Batting: 57" × 57"

CUTTING

WOF is width of fabric. • *Refer to Cutting Diamonds (page 11) for more information about creating diamond shapes.*

Dark red

• Cut 4 strips 2½" × WOF.

• Cut 5 strips 1½" × WOF for second inner border; sew together, end to end, and subcut:

2 strips 1½" × 44"

2 strips 1½" × 46"

Light red

• Cut 2 strips 2½" × WOF.

Dark green

• Cut 4 strips 2½" × WOF.

Light green

• Cut 4 strips 2½" × WOF.

Black

• Cut 2 strips 13¼" × WOF; subcut 4 squares 13¼" × 13¼" and cut diagonally once for a total of 8 large triangles.

• Cut 1 strip 9½" × WOF; subcut 4 squares 9½" × 9½" and cut diagonally once for a total of 8 small triangles.

• Cut 4 strips 3½" × WOF; subcut 24 diamonds 3½" wide.

• Cut 10 strips 2½" × WOF for strip sets.

• Cut 5 strips 1¾" × WOF for outer border; sew together, end to end, and subcut:

2 strips 1¾" × 46"

2 strips 1¾" × 48½"

Binding

• Cut 5 strips 2¼" × WOF.

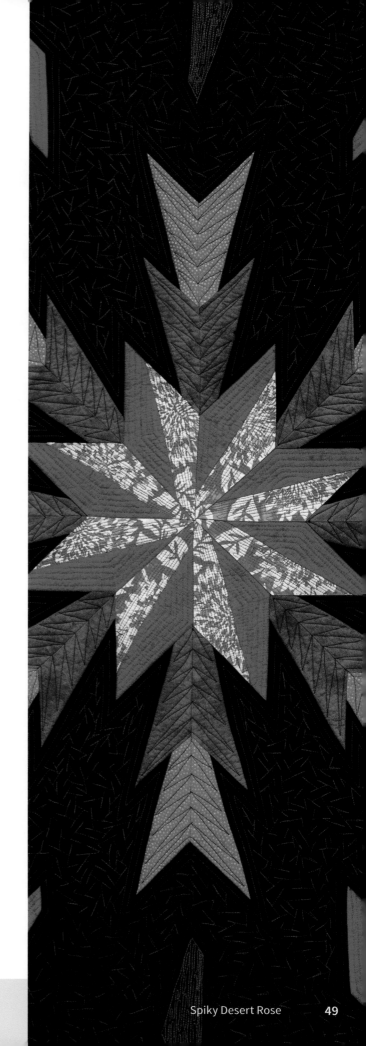

Making the Split Diamonds

1. Following the instructions for Creating a Strip Set (page 11), sew the strips together as shown. Press the seams toward the darker fabrics.

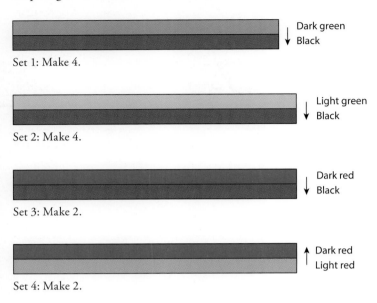

Set 1: Make 4.

Dark green
↓ Black

Set 2: Make 4.

Light green
↓ Black

Set 3: Make 2.

Dark red
↓ Black

Set 4: Make 2.

↑ Dark red
Light red

2. Make templates from the 3½″ diamond A and 3½″ diamond Ar patterns (page 93). (Refer to Cutting from Templates, page 10, for more information about making and using templates.)

3. Following the instructions for Cutting Split Diamonds (page 13), cut 8 split diamonds from each of the strip sets, using template A. Label A diamonds.

4. From strip sets 1 and 2, cut 8 split diamonds each, using template Ar (reverse). Label Ar diamonds.

Making the Large Diamonds

1. Piece 8 large diamonds, using black diamonds and split diamonds as shown.

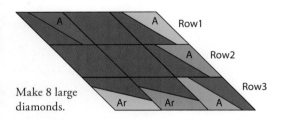

Make 8 large diamonds.

2. Arrange the 8 large diamonds with the 8 large and 8 small black triangles to make 4 A and 4 B triangle units. (Refer to Basic Piecing Order, page 15, for more information.) Sew together as shown.

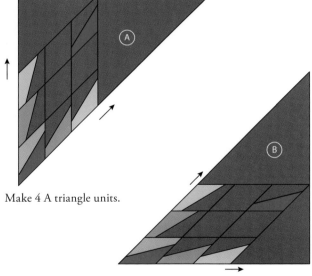

Make 4 A triangle units.

Make 4 B triangle units.

Assembling and Finishing the Quilt

1. Arrange A and B triangle units. (Refer to Basic Piecing Order, page 15, for more information.) Sew together as shown.

Sew according to diagram.

2. Refer to the quilt assembly diagram to add borders.

Quilt assembly

3. Use your favorite methods to layer, quilt, and bind the quilt with the binding strips. (Refer to Quiltmaking Basics: How to Finish Your Quilt, page 87, for more detailed information.)

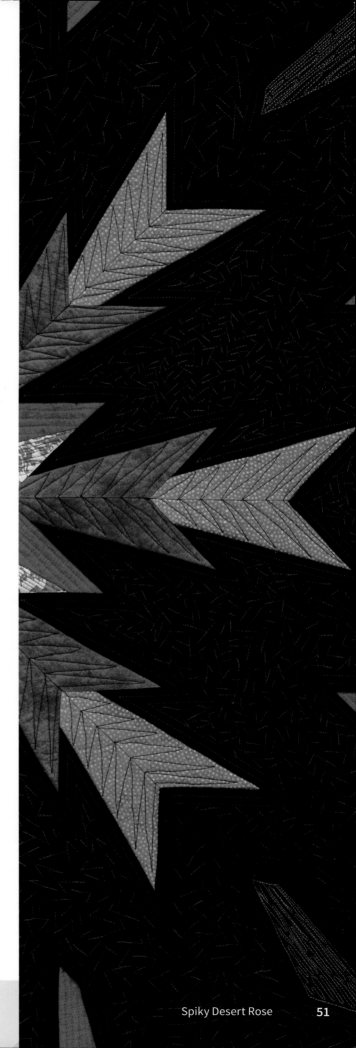

Rotating Stars

FINISHED QUILT: 96″ × 96″ ♦ 5 × 5 diamond layout

This quilt is made of three eight-pointed stars that all have the same large diamond pattern. What makes the center star look different from the edge stars is the eight large diamonds that are rotated end over end—what was the outer point becomes the center star. The design completely changes into a feathered star! Two of the stars are pieced in halves and placed on the edges of the quilt, creating a modern look.

MATERIALS

Yardage is based on 42"-wide fabric.

Light blue: ¼ yard

Medium blue: ⅓ yard

Blue: ⅓ yard

Dark blue: ½ yard

Light gray: ¼ yard

Medium gray: ⅓ yard

Gray: ⅓ yard

Black: ½ yard

Light orange: ¼ yard

Medium orange: ⅓ yard

Orange: ⅓ yard

Dark orange: ½ yard

Cream: 11¼ yards

Binding: 1 yard

Backing: 104" × 104"

Batting: 104" × 104"

CUTTING

WOF is width of fabric. • *LOF is length of fabric.*

Refer to Cutting Diamonds (page 11) for more information about creating diamond shapes.

Center Star 1

Measures 48½" × 48½". *Label all pieces Star 1.*

Light blue
• Cut 1 strip 1¾" × WOF.

Medium blue
• Cut 1 strip 2½" × WOF; subcut 8 diamonds 2½" wide.

Blue
• Cut 1 strip 2½" × WOF; subcut 8 diamonds 2½" wide.

Dark blue
• Cut 1 strip 1¾" × WOF.
• Cut 1 strip 2½" × WOF; subcut 8 diamonds 2½" wide.

Light gray
• Cut 2 strips 1¾" × WOF.

Medium gray
• Cut 2 strips 1¾" × WOF.

Gray
• Cut 2 strips 1¾" × WOF.

Black
• Cut 2 strips 1¾" × WOF.

Cream
• Cut a length of fabric 2⅝ yards (94½") × WOF; set aside.
• Cut 2 strips 15" × WOF; subcut 4 squares 15" × 15" and cut diagonally once for a total of 8 large triangles.
• Cut 2 strips 11" × WOF; subcut 4 squares 11" × 11" and cut diagonally once for a total of 8 small triangles.
• Cut 11 strips 2½" × WOF; subcut 104 diamonds 2½" wide.
• Cut 8 strips 1¾" × WOF.

Edge Star 2

Each half measures 48½" × 24½". *Label all pieces Star 2.*

Medium gray
• Cut 1 strip 2½" × WOF; subcut 8 diamonds 2½" wide.

Gray
• Cut 1 strip 2½" × WOF; subcut 8 diamonds 2½" wide.

Black
• Cut 1 strip 1¾" × WOF.
• Cut 1 strip 2½" × WOF; subcut 8 diamonds 2½" wide.

Light orange
• Cut 2 strips 1¾" × WOF.

Cutting continued →

Medium orange

- Cut 2 strips 1¾″ × WOF.

Orange

- Cut 2 strips 1¾″ × WOF.

Dark orange

- Cut 2 strips 1¾″ × WOF.

Cream

- Cut 2 strips 15″ × WOF; subcut 4 squares 15″ × 15″ and cut diagonally once for a total of 8 large triangles.
- Cut 2 strips 11″ × WOF; subcut 4 squares 11″ × 11″ and cut diagonally once for a total of 8 small triangles.
- Cut 11 strips 2½″ × WOF; subcut 104 diamonds 2½″ wide.
- Cut 9 strips 1¾″ × WOF.

Edge Star 3

Each half measures 48½″ × 24½″. *Label all pieces Star 3.*

Medium orange

- Cut 1 strip 2½″ × WOF; subcut 8 diamonds 2½″ wide.

Orange

- Cut 1 strip 2½″ × WOF; subcut 8 diamonds 2½″ wide.

Dark orange

- Cut 1 strip 1¾″ × WOF.
- Cut 1 strip 2½″ × WOF; subcut 8 diamonds 2½″ wide.

Light blue

- Cut 2 strips 1¾″ × WOF.

Medium blue

- Cut 2 strips 1¾″ × WOF.

Blue

- Cut 2 strips 1¾″ × WOF.

Dark blue

- Cut 2 strips 1¾″ × WOF.

Cream

- Cut 2 strips 15″ × WOF; subcut 4 squares 15″ × 15″ and cut diagonally once for a total of 8 triangles.
- Cut 2 strips 11″ × WOF; subcut 4 squares 11″ × 11″ and cut diagonally once for a total of 8 triangles.
- Cut 11 strips 2½″ × WOF; subcut 104 diamonds 2½″ wide.
- Cut 9 strips 1¾″ × WOF.

Background

Cream

Use the 2⅝-yard cut set aside previously for the following LOF cuts.

- Cut 1 strip 20½″ × LOF; subcut 4 squares 20½″ × 20½″.
- Cut 2 strips 4½″ × LOF; subcut 4 strips 4½″ × 44½″.

Binding

- Cut 12 strips 2¼″ × WOF.

Making the Split Diamonds for Center Star 1

1. Following the instructions for Creating a Strip Set (page 11), sew the following strip sets together using 1¾″ × WOF strips. Press the seams toward the darker fabrics.

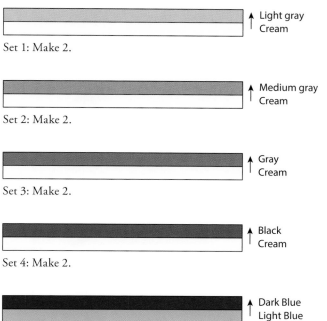

Set 1: Make 2.

Set 2: Make 2.

Set 3: Make 2.

Set 4: Make 2.

Set 5: Make 1.

2. Make templates from the 2½″ diamond B and 2½″ diamond Br patterns (page 94). (Refer to Cutting from Templates, page 10, for more information about making and using templates.)

3. Following the instructions for Cutting Split Diamonds (page 13), cut 8 split diamonds from each of strip sets 1–5, using template B. Label B diamonds.

4. From each of strip sets 1–4, cut another 8 split diamonds, using template Br (reverse). Label Br diamonds.

Making the Split Diamonds for Edge Star 2

1. Following the instructions for Creating a Strip Set (page 11), sew the following strip sets together using 1¾″ × WOF strips. Press the seams toward the darker fabrics.

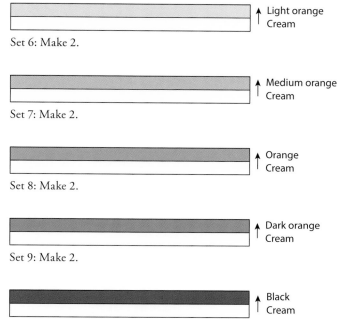

Set 6: Make 2.

Set 7: Make 2.

Set 8: Make 2.

Set 9: Make 2.

Set 10: Make 1.

2. Make templates from the 2½″ diamond B and 2½″ diamond Br patterns (page 94). (Refer to Cutting from Templates, page 10, for more information about making and using templates.)

3. Following the instructions for Cutting Split Diamonds (page 13), cut 8 split diamonds from each of strip sets 6–10, using template B. Label B diamonds.

4. From each of strip sets 6–9, cut another 8 split diamonds, using template Br (reverse). Label Br diamonds.

Making the Split Diamonds for Edge Star 3

1. Following the instructions for Creating a Strip Set (page 11), sew the following strip sets using 1¾″ × WOF strips. Press the seams toward the darker fabrics.

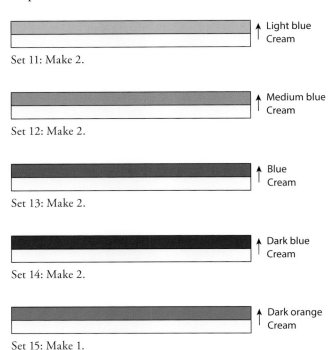

↑ Light blue
↑ Cream

Set 11: Make 2.

↑ Medium blue
↑ Cream

Set 12: Make 2.

↑ Blue
↑ Cream

Set 13: Make 2.

↑ Dark blue
↑ Cream

Set 14: Make 2.

↑ Dark orange
↑ Cream

Set 15: Make 1.

2. Following the instructions for Cutting Split Diamonds (page 13), cut 8 split diamonds from each of strip sets 11–15, using template B. Label B diamonds.

3. From each of strip sets 11–14, cut another 8 split diamonds, using template Br (reverse). Label Br diamonds.

Making the Large Diamonds and Stars

1. The stars are made of 8 large diamonds each. Follow the diagrams for placement of the split diamonds and solid diamonds. Sew the diamonds in rows; then sew the rows together. Press according to the arrows.

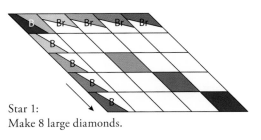

Star 1:
Make 8 large diamonds.

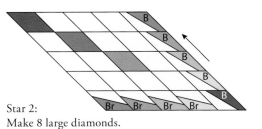

Star 2:
Make 8 large diamonds.

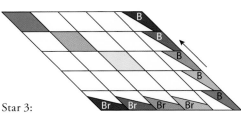

Star 3:
Make 8 large diamonds.

2. Arrange the 8 large diamonds with the 8 large and 8 small cream triangles to make 4 A and 4 B triangle units. (Refer to Basic Piecing Order, page 15, for more information.) Sew together as shown.

Star 1: Make complete star.

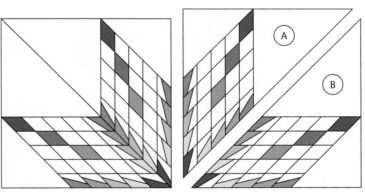

Star 2: Make 2 half-stars.

Star 3: Make 2 half-stars.

Assembling and Finishing the Quilt

This quilt is sewn together with partial seams. This is when you sew part of a seam but you don't finish the seam. Then after you sew another seam, you come back and finish sewing the partial seam. The seams in this quilt are labeled in the diagram.

1. Arrange the 1 full and 4 half-stars with the 4 squares 20½″ × 20½″ and the 4 strips 4½″ × 44½″. Sew the seams in numerical order in the direction of the arrows and move counterclockwise around the outside of the quilt. Seams 1, 4, 7, and 10 are the partial seams that *stop* at a red dot. Seams 13, 14, 15, 16, and 17 are partial seams that *begin* at a red dot. These last 5 seams are sewn in a clockwise direction.

Quilt assembly

2. Use your favorite methods to layer, quilt, and bind the quilt with the binding strips. (Refer to Quiltmaking Basics: How to Finish Your Quilt, page 87, for more detailed information.)

QUILTS MADE WITH LARGE STAR POINTS OUTSIDE THE EIGHT-POINTED STAR

In this section, the eight-pointed stars have additional design elements on their backgrounds. Extra star points and border piecing all add style beyond the stars. Enjoy creating these elements in *Christmas Cactus* (page 61), *Blue Cactus* (page 66), and *Let's Go Hunting* (page 71).

Making Star Points

1. Make 2 copies of the Large Star Points patterns C and D (page 95). Trim the D portion off of 1 copy to create template C. Cut around the complete triangle shape of the second copy to make template D. Template D is the size of the star points. The flipped template will give you the reverse image (Dr). (Refer to Cutting from Templates, page 10, and Cutting the D Shapes, page 10, for more information about how to make and use templates.)

2. Use template C to trim away the background area of the large and small background triangles where star points will be sewn in. Flip template C as needed to make the correct cuts. Orient the template in relation to the right angle of each triangle as shown in the diagrams.

3. From the dark fabric cut a 3¾″ × WOF strip; subcut template D shapes.

4. From the light fabric cut a 3¾″ × WOF strip; subcut template D-reverse (Dr) shapes.

5. Position the D pieces where the C piece was trimmed off. It is easy to get mixed up on the position of the triangles. Study the diagram to make sure the positions are correct.

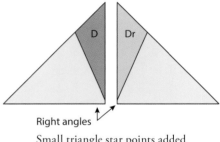

Small triangle star points added

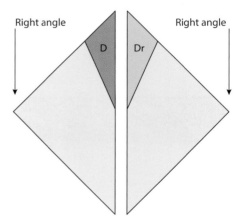

Large triangle star points added

Christmas Cactus

FINISHED QUILT: 48″ × 48″ ♦ 5 × 5 diamond layout

Note there is a star inside of a star in this quilt, which is created by changing the diamond colors. This same look is also found in *Echo Star* (page 28). The split diamonds create the prickly red star inside the middle of the quilt.

MATERIALS

Yardage is based on 42"-wide fabric.

Light red: ½ yard

Medium red: ¼ yard

Red: ½ yard

Dark red: ¼ yard

Green: ⅔ yard

Black: 1 yard

Light gray: 2 yards

Binding: ½ yard

Backing: 56" × 56"

Batting: 56" × 56"

CUTTING

WOF is width of fabric.

Refer to Cutting Diamonds (page 11), Cutting Long Diamonds (page 11), and Cutting the D Shapes (page 10) for more information about creating these three types of diamonds.

Light red

- Cut 2 strips 1¾" × WOF.
- Cut 2 strips 3¾" × WOF; subcut 8 template D shapes. Label D.

Medium red

- Cut 3 strips 1¾" × WOF.

Red

- Cut 2 strips 1¾" × WOF.
- Cut 2 strips 3¾" × WOF; subcut 8 template Dr (reverse) shapes. Label Dr.

Dark red

- Cut 2 strips 1¾" × WOF.

Green

- Cut 4 strips 1¾" × WOF.
- Cut 5 strips 2½" × WOF; subcut:
  8 diamonds 2½" wide
  8 long right diamonds 2½" × 4½"
  8 long left diamonds 2½" × 6½"

Black

- Cut 5 strips 1¾" × WOF.
- Cut 8 strips 2½" × WOF; subcut:
  8 diamonds 2½" wide
  8 long left diamonds 2½" × 4½"
  8 long right diamonds 2½" × 6½"
  8 long left diamonds 2½" × 8½

Light gray

- Cut 2 strips 15" × WOF; subcut 4 squares 15" × 15" and cut diagonally once for a total of 8 large triangles.
- Cut 2 strips 11" × WOF; subcut 4 squares 11" × 11" and cut diagonally once for a total of 8 small triangles.

Binding

- Cut 6 strips 2¼" × WOF.

Making the Split Diamonds

1. Following the instructions for Creating a Strip Set (page 11), sew strips together using 1¾″ × WOF strips. Press the seams toward the darker fabrics.

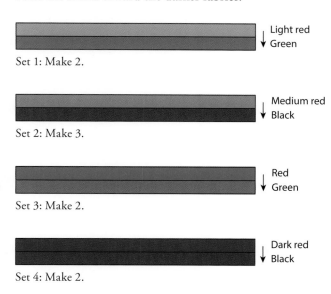

Set 1: Make 2. — Light red / Green

Set 2: Make 3. — Medium red / Black

Set 3: Make 2. — Red / Green

Set 4: Make 2. — Dark red / Black

2. Make templates from the 2½″ diamond B and 2½″ diamond Br patterns (page 94). (Refer to Cutting from Templates, page 10, for more information about making and using templates.)

3. Following the instructions for Cutting Split Diamonds (page 13), cut 8 split diamonds from strip sets 1, 3, and 4, and cut 16 split diamonds from strip set 2, using template B. Label B diamonds.

4. In addition, cut 8 split diamonds from strip sets 1–4, using template Br (reverse). Label Br diamonds.

Making the Large Diamonds

The star is made of 8 large diamonds. Follow the diagram for placement of the split diamonds and solid diamonds. Sew the diamonds in rows; then sew rows together. Press according to the arrows.

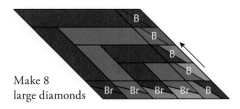

Make 8 large diamonds

Making the Large Star Points

1. Following the instructions for Making Star Points (page 60), use template C to cut off corners of the small and large light gray triangles.

2. Sew D and D-reverse (Dr) pieces to the large gray triangles.

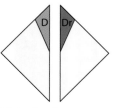

Make 4 each.

3. Sew D and D-reverse (Dr) pieces to the small gray triangles.

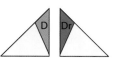

Make 4 each.

4. Use a large diamond, large triangle, and small triangle to make 4 A and 4 B triangle units. (Refer to Basic Piecing Order, page 15, for more information.) Notice that in both A and B triangle units, the light red D unit is to the left, red Dr unit to the right of the diamond point, regardless of the triangle's size.

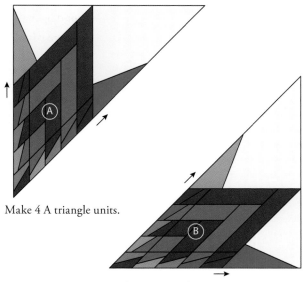

Make 4 A triangle units.

Make 4 B triangle units.

Assembling and Finishing the Quilt

1. Sew together the 8 large triangle units, alternating A and B. (Refer to Basic Piecing Order, page 15, for more information.)

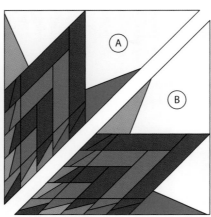

Quilt assembly

2. Use your favorite methods to layer, quilt, and bind the quilt with the binding strips. (Refer to Quiltmaking Basics: How to Finish Your Quilt, page 87, for more detailed information.)

Blue Cactus

FINISHED QUILT: 48″ × 48″ ♦ 5 × 5 diamond layout

Blue Cactus gives the impression that several stars are stacked on top of each other. The dark navy star on top looks as if it is allowing you a peek through its center to view the star below; red cactus-like leaves shoot out from behind it, going from light to dark, creating movement and radiating like a flare.

MATERIALS

Yardage is based on 42"-wide fabric.

Light blue: ¾ yard

Blue: ¾ yard

Light red: ¼ yard

Medium red: ¼ yard

Dark red: ¼ yard

Navy: 1¼ yards

Gray: 2 yards

Binding: ½ yard

Backing: 56″ × 56″

Batting: 56″ × 56″

CUTTING

WOF is width of fabric. • *Refer to Cutting Diamonds (page 11) and Cutting Long Diamonds (page 11) for more information about creating diamond shapes.*

Make 2 templates from the Large Star Points C and D pattern (page 95). (Refer to Cutting from Templates, page 10, and Cutting the D Shapes, page 10, for more information about making and using templates.)

Light blue

• Cut 2 strips 3¾″ × WOF; subcut 8 template D-reverse shapes. Label D-reverse.

• Cut 3 strips 2½″ × WOF; subcut:
  4 diamonds 2½″ wide
  8 long right diamonds* (2½″ × 4½″)

• Cut 2 strips 1¾″ × WOF.

Blue

• Cut 1 strip 3¾″ × WOF; subcut 8 template D shapes. Label D.

• Cut 3 strips 2½″ × WOF; subcut:
  4 diamonds 2½″ wide
  8 long left diamonds* (2½″ × 4½″)

• Cut 2 strips 1¾″ × WOF.

Light red

• Cut 2 strips 1¾″ × WOF.

Medium red

• Cut 3 strips 1¾″ × WOF.

Dark red

• Cut 3 strips 1¾″ × WOF.

Navy

• Cut 2 strips 4½″ × WOF; subcut 8 diamonds 4½″ wide.

• Cut 3 strips 2½″ × WOF; subcut 24 diamonds 2½″ wide.

• Cut 4 strips 2½″ × WOF; subcut:
  8 long left diamonds* (2½″ × 6½″)
  8 long right diamonds* (2½″ × 6½″)

• Cut 2 strips 1¾″ × WOF.

Gray

• Cut 2 strips 15″ × WOF; subcut 4 squares 15″ × 15″ and cut diagonally once for a total of 8 large triangles.

• Cut 2 strips 11″ × WOF; subcut 4 squares 11″ × 11″ and cut diagonally once for a total of 8 small triangles.

Binding

• Cut 5 strips 2¼″ × WOF.

* For a visual of these shapes, see Cutting Long Diamonds (page 11).

Making the Split Diamonds

1. Make templates from the 2½″ diamond B and 2½″ diamond Br patterns (page 94). (Refer to Cutting from Templates, page 10, for more information about making and using templates.)

2. Following the instructions for Creating a Strip Set (page 11), sew the following strip sets using 1¾″ × WOF strips. Press the seams toward the darker fabrics.

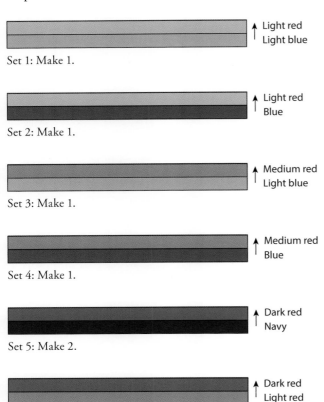

Set 1: Make 1. — Light red / Light blue

Set 2: Make 1. — Light red / Blue

Set 3: Make 1. — Medium red / Light blue

Set 4: Make 1. — Medium red / Blue

Set 5: Make 2. — Dark red / Navy

Set 6: Make 1. — Dark red / Light red

3. Following the instructions for Cutting Split Diamonds (page 13), cut 8 split diamonds from each strip set 1, 3, 5, and 6, using template B. Label B diamonds.

4. From each strip set 2, 4, and 5, cut 8 split diamonds, using template Br. Label Br diamonds.

Making the Large Diamonds

1. The star is made of 8 large diamonds. Follow the diagram for placement of the split diamonds, solid diamonds, and long right and left diamonds. Make 4 with a light blue center diamond and 4 with a blue center diamond. Sew the diamonds together in alphabetical order. Press according to the arrows.

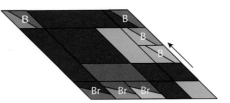

4 large diamonds with a light blue center diamond

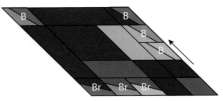

4 large diamonds with a blue center diamond

Making the Large Star Points

1. Following the instructions for Making Star Points (page 60), use template C to cut off corners of the light gray triangles.

2. Sew D and D-reverse (Dr) pieces to the large gray triangles.

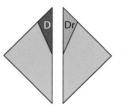

Make 4 each.

3. Sew D and D-reverse (Dr) pieces to the small gray triangles.

Make 4 each.

4. Use a large diamond, large triangle, and small triangle to make 4 A and 4 B triangle units. (Refer to Basic Piecing Order, page 15, for more information.) Notice that in both A and B triangle units, the dark D unit is to the left and the light D unit is to the right of the diamond point, regardless of the triangle's size.

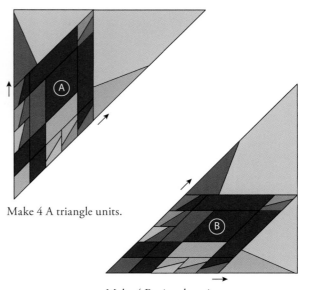

Make 4 A triangle units.

Make 4 B triangle units.

Assembling and Finishing the Quilt

1. Sew together the 8 triangle units, alternating A and B. (Refer to Basic Piecing Order, page 15, for more information.)

Quilt assembly

2. Use your favorite methods to layer, quilt, and bind the quilt with the binding strips. (Refer to Quiltmaking Basics: How to Finish Your Quilt, page 87, for more detailed information.)

Let's Go Hunting

FINISHED QUILT: 48″ × 48″ without border / 64″ × 64″ with border ♦ 5 × 5 diamond layout

Let's Go Hunting is a 48″ × 48″ star before the two borders are added. The basic directions are for the star only. I have included the border options separately. If you choose to add these borders to another quilt, it will be easy to do so—look for the places in the instructions for border information identified as "Border option."

MATERIALS

Yardage is based on 42"-wide fabric.

Light green: ¾ yard

Dark green: ¾ yard

Light orange: ¼ yard
Border option: + ¼ yard

Medium orange: ¼ yard
Border option: + ¼ yard

Orange: ¼ yard
Border option: + ¼ yard

Dark orange: ¼ yard
Border option: + ¼ yard

Light brown: ⅓ yard

Dark brown: ⅔ yard

Cream: 2 yards
Border option: + 2½ yards

Binding: ½ yard
Border option: + ¼ yard

Backing: 56" × 56"
Border option: 72" × 72"

Batting: 56" × 56"
Border option: 72" × 72"

CUTTING

WOF is width of fabric. • LOF is length of fabric.

Refer to Cutting Diamonds (page 11) for more information about creating diamond shapes.

Make 2 templates from the Large Star Points C and D pattern (page 95). (Refer to Cutting from Templates, page 10, and Cutting the D Shapes, page 10, for more information about making and using templates.)

Light green

- Cut 4 strips 1¾" × WOF.
- Cut 5 strips 2½" × WOF; subcut 48 diamonds 2½" wide.

Dark green

- Cut 4 strips 1¾" × WOF.
- Cut 5 strips 2½" × WOF; subcut 48 diamonds 2½" wide.

Light orange

- Cut 2 strips 1¾" × WOF.
- *Border option: Cut 4 strips 1¾" × WOF.*

Medium orange

- Cut 1 strip 2½" × WOF; subcut 4 diamonds 2½" wide.
- Cut 2 strips 1¾" × WOF.
- *Border option: Cut 4 strips 1¾" × WOF.*

Orange

- Cut 2 strips 1¾" × WOF.
- *Border option: Cut 3 strips 1¾" × WOF.*

Dark orange

- Cut 1 strip 2½" × WOF; subcut 4 diamonds 2½" wide.
- Cut 2 strips 1¾" × WOF.
- *Border option: Cut 3 strips 1¾" × WOF.*

Light brown

- Cut 2 strips 3¾" × WOF; subcut 8 template D-reverse (Dr) shapes. Label Dr.

Dark brown

- Cut 2 strips 3¾" × WOF; subcut 8 template D shapes. Label D.
- Cut 4 strips 2½" × WOF; subcut 32 diamonds 2½" wide.

Cream

- Cut 2 strips 15" × WOF; subcut 4 squares 15" × 15" and cut diagonally once for a total of 8 large triangles.
- Cut 2 strips 11" × WOF; subcut 4 squares 11" × 11" and cut diagonally once for a total of 8 small triangles.

Cream for border option

- From the 1⅝ yards (58½") × WOF rectangle, cut 6 strips 4½" × LOF; subcut:

  2 strips 4½" × 56½" for top and bottom inner borders

  2 strips 4½" × 48½" for side inner borders

  2 strips 4½" × 30½" for arrow border

  2 strips 4½" × 20½" for arrow border

  2 squares 4½" × 4½" for arrow border corners

- Cut 1 strip 2⅞" × WOF; subcut 8 squares 2⅞" × 2⅞" and cut diagonally once for a total of 16 triangles. Label Z.

- Cut 14 strips 1¾" × WOF.

Binding

- Cut 6 strips 2¼" × WOF.
- *Border option: Cut 8 additional strips 2¼" × WOF.*

Making the Split Diamonds

1. Following the instructions for Creating a Strip Set (page 11), sew the following strip sets together using 1¾″ × WOF strips. Press the seams toward the darker fabrics.

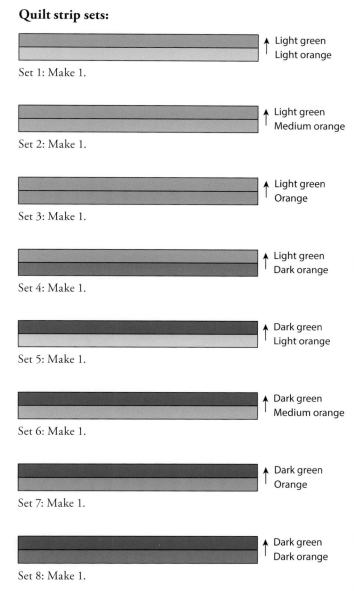

Quilt strip sets:

Set 1: Make 1. — ↑ Light green / Light orange

Set 2: Make 1. — ↑ Light green / Medium orange

Set 3: Make 1. — ↑ Light green / Orange

Set 4: Make 1. — ↑ Light green / Dark orange

Set 5: Make 1. — ↑ Dark green / Light orange

Set 6: Make 1. — ↑ Dark green / Medium orange

Set 7: Make 1. — ↑ Dark green / Orange

Set 8: Make 1. — ↑ Dark green / Dark orange

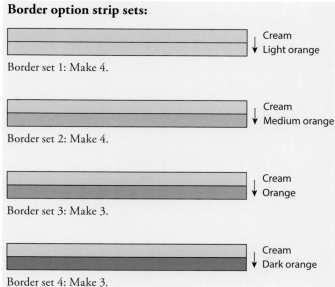

Border option strip sets:

Border set 1: Make 4. — ↓ Cream / Light orange

Border set 2: Make 4. — ↓ Cream / Medium orange

Border set 3: Make 3. — ↓ Cream / Orange

Border set 4: Make 3. — ↓ Cream / Dark orange

2. Make templates from the 2½″ diamond B and 2½″ diamond Br patterns (page 94). (Refer to Cutting from Templates, page 10, for more information about making and using templates.)

3. Following the instructions for Cutting Split Diamonds (page 13), cut 8 split diamonds from each of strip sets 1–4, using template Br. Label Br diamonds.

4. From each of strip sets 5–8, cut 8 split diamonds using template B. Label B diamonds.

5. *Border option:* From border strip sets 1 and 2, cut 12 split diamonds each. From border strip sets 3 and 4, cut 10 split diamonds each, using template B. Label B diamonds.

6. *Border option:* Repeat Step 5 using template Br. Label Br diamonds.

Making the Large Diamonds

The star is made of 8 large diamonds. The 4 A diamonds have a dark orange center diamond; the 4 B diamonds have a medium orange center diamond. (Refer to Basic Piecing Order, page 15, for detailed information.) Follow the diagram for placement of the split diamonds and solid diamonds. Sew the diamonds in rows; then sew rows together. Press according to the arrows.

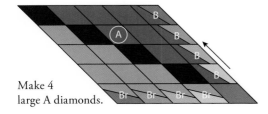

Make 4
large A diamonds.

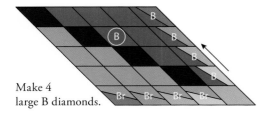

Make 4
large B diamonds.

Making the Large Star Points

1. Following the instructions for Making Star Points (page 60), use template C to cut off corners of the cream triangles.

2. Sew D and D-reverse (Dr) pieces to the large cream triangles.

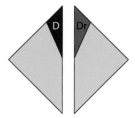

Make 4 each.

3. Sew D and D-reverse (Dr) pieces to the small cream triangles.

Make 4 each.

4. Use a large diamond, large triangle, and small triangle to make 4 A and 4 B triangle units. (Refer to Basic Piecing Order, page 15, for more information.) Notice that in both A and B triangle units, the dark D unit is to the left and light D is to the right of the diamond point, regardless of the triangle's size.

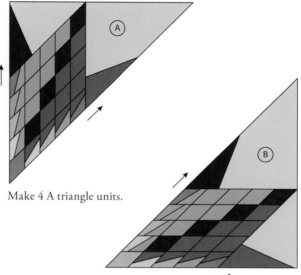

Make 4 A triangle units.

Make 4 B triangle units.

Assembling the Quilt

1. Sew together the 8 triangle units, alternating A and B.

(Refer to Basic Piecing Order, page 15, for more information.)

Quilt center assembly

2. If you choose to add the additional arrow borders, continue to the next section.

If you choose *not* to add the optional borders, skip to Finishing the Quilt (page 78).

Border Option: Making and Adding Arrow Borders

1. Sew diamond chains as shown. Each top row will be made of B diamonds and each bottom row will be made of Br diamonds. Add a half-square triangle Z of cream to both ends of the rows.

Make 2 borders with 10 complete arrows.

Make 2 borders with 12 complete arrows.

2. Sew top and bottom rows together to make arrow unit. Make 4 total.

3. Add a 4½″ × 20½″ strip to the "pointed" end of each 12-diamond unit. Add a 4½″ × 30½″ strip to the "pointed" end of each 10-diamond unit.

4. Follow the diagram for adding borders to the quilt.

Border assembly (*optional*)

Finishing the Quilt

Use your favorite methods to layer, quilt, and bind the quilt with the binding strips. (Refer to Quiltmaking Basics: How to Finish Your Quilt, page 87, for more detailed information.)

QUILTS MADE WITH ADDITIONAL APPLIQUÉ EMBELLISHMENT

Another design element that can be used as a frame for the eight-pointed star is the appliquéd zigzag ribbon. It makes an eye-catching addition to a stunning diamond star.

Faceted Winter Star

FINISHED QUILT: 48″ × 48″ ♦ 4 × 4 diamond layout

An added feature for this star is the blue zigzag strip that forms an octagon around the star. The shiny silver fabric is a lamé with a stabilizer added to the back.

MATERIALS

Yardage is based on 42"-wide fabric.

Light blue: ½ yard

Light/medium blue: ½ yard

Medium blue: ½ yard

Medium/dark blue: 1 yard

Dark blue: ¼ yard

Navy: 1¼ yards

Silver lamé: ⅜ yard

White with silver sparkle: 2¼ yards

Binding: ½ yard

Backing: 54" × 54"

Batting: 54" × 54"

Double-sided fusible web: 1¼ yards

Fabric stabilizer: ⅜ yard

Card stock or poster board: 1 sheet

CUTTING

WOF is width of fabric. • *Refer to Cutting Diamonds (page 11) for more information about creating diamond shapes.*

Light blue
- Cut 6 strips 1¾" × WOF.

Light/medium blue
- Cut 1 strip 1¾" × WOF.
- Cut 2 strips 2½" × WOF; subcut 16 diamonds 2½" wide.

Medium blue
- Cut 3 strips 2½" × WOF; subcut 24 diamonds 2½" wide.

Medium/dark blue
- Cut 2 strips 2½" × WOF; subcut 16 diamonds 2½" wide.
- Cut 1 strip 12" × WOF.

Dark blue
- Cut 1 strip 2½" × WOF; subcut 8 diamonds 2½" wide.

Navy
- Cut 6 strips 1¾" × WOF.
- Cut 1 strip 12" × WOF.

Silver lamé

Apply stabilizer according to manufacturer instructions before cutting.

- Cut 1 strip 1¾" × WOF.
- Cut 1 strip 2½" × WOF; subcut 8 diamonds 2½" wide.

White with silver sparkle
- Cut 2 strips 12" × WOF; subcut 4 squares 12" × 12" and cut diagonally once for a total of 8 large triangles.
- Cut 2 strips 9" × WOF; subcut 4 squares 9" × 9" and cut diagonally once for a total of 8 small triangles.
- Cut 5 strips 5½" × WOF.

Binding
- Cut 5 strips 2¼" × WOF.

Double-sided fusible web
- Cut 1 strip 12" × 42".

Making the Split Diamonds

1. Following the instructions for Creating a Strip Set (page 11), sew strip sets together using 1¾" × WOF strips. Press the seams toward the darker fabrics.

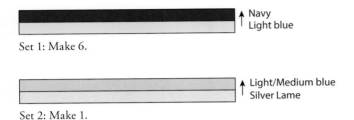

Set 1: Make 6.

Set 2: Make 1.

2. Make templates from the 2½" diamond B and 2½" diamond Br patterns (page 94). (Refer to Cutting from Templates, page 10, for more information about making and using templates.)

3. Following the instructions for Cutting Split Diamonds (page 13), cut 24 split diamonds from strip set 1, and 8 split diamonds from strip set 2, using template B. Label B diamonds.

4. From strip set 1, cut another 24 split diamonds, using template Br (reverse). Label Br diamonds.

Making the Large Diamonds

1. The star is made of 8 large diamonds. Follow the diagram for placement of the split diamonds and solid diamonds. Sew the diamonds in rows; then sew rows together. Press according to the arrows.

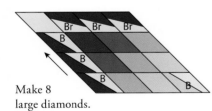

Make 8 large diamonds.

2. Arrange the 8 triangle units with 8 large and 8 small white triangles to make 4 A and 4 B triangle units. (Refer to Basic Piecing Order, page 15, for more information.) Sew together as shown.

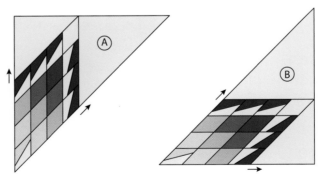

Make 4 A triangle units.   Make 4 B triangle units.

Assembling the Quilt

1. Sew together the 8 triangle units. (Refer to Basic Piecing Order, page 15, for more information.)

2. Starting with the 2 shorter strips, add border strips to the sides of the quilt first.

Quilt assembly

MAKING THE ZIGZAG

This zigzag is created by making a double-sided piece of fabric. This is achieved by pressing 2 different fabrics to a double-sided fusible web strip. From this double-sided fabric, you will cut strips to make the zigzag.

1. Press the navy 12″ × WOF strip to the fusible web. Follow the manufacturer's directions for applying the web. Peel off the paper from the back of the piece and press the medium/dark blue 12″ × WOF strip to the remaining side. Cut 8 strips ¾″ × WOF.

2. From the card stock, cut a 1¼″ × 11″ strip, or if using poster board, cut a 1¼″ × 36″ strip. Mark parallel lines on a 45° angle 1¼″ apart.

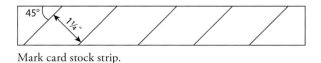

Mark card stock strip.

3. Spray the double-sided fabric strips with spray starch.

4. Wrap the double-sided fabric around the card stock or poster board, matching the edge of the fabric with the parallel lines. Press on both sides of card stock until dry. Let cool, and then slide the card stock or poster board out from between the wrapped fabric.

5. Repeat Step 4 until the strip is completely ironed.

6. Position on the quilt top as shown. (I centered the zigzag on the 4 borders.) Pin into position on the quilt at every zig and every zag. Hide any "joins" behind the navy fabric sections.

7. Use a monofilament thread and zigzag stitch along the raw edges using a stitch length of 1 mm and a width of 2 mm.

Finishing the Quilt

1. Use your favorite methods to layer, quilt, and bind the quilt with the binding strips. (Refer to Quiltmaking Basics: How to Finish Your Quilt, page 87, for more detailed information.)

2. To tie the winter wonderland theme into the quilt, I quilted snowflakes with loops in the background.

QUILTMAKING BASICS: HOW TO FINISH YOUR QUILT

General Guidelines

SEAM ALLOWANCES

A ¼″ seam allowance is used for most projects. It's a good idea to do a test seam before you begin sewing to check that your ¼″ is accurate. Accuracy is the key to successful piecing.

There is generally no need to backstitch. Ordinarily, seamlines will be crossed by another seam, which will anchor them.

PRESSING

In general, press the seams toward the darker fabric. Press lightly in an up-and-down motion. Avoid using a very hot iron or over-ironing, which can distort shapes and blocks. Be especially careful when pressing bias edges, as they stretch easily.

Borders

When border strips are cut on the crosswise grain, piece the strips together to achieve the needed lengths.

In most cases, the side borders are sewn on first. When you have finished the quilt top, measure it through the center vertically. This will be the length to cut the side borders. Place pins at the centers of all four sides of the quilt top, as well as in the center of each side border strip. Pin the side borders to the quilt top first, matching the center pins. Using a ¼″ seam allowance, sew the borders to the quilt top and press toward border.

Measure horizontally across the center of the quilt top, including the side borders. This will be the length to cut the top and bottom borders. Repeat, pinning, sewing, and pressing.

Backing

You'll notice in the materials lists, there are no yardage amounts listed for backings. Instead, the size of the backing is given. Generally, it is a minimum of 8″ longer and wider than the quilt top. To economize, plan on piecing the back from any of the generous leftover quilting fabrics from the project or from blocks in your collection. Trim the selvages before you piece to the desired size.

Batting

The type of batting to use is a personal decision; consult your local quilt shop. Cut batting approximately 8″ longer and wider than your quilt top. Note that your batting choice will affect how much quilting is necessary for the quilt. Check the manufacturer's instructions to see how far apart the quilting lines can be.

Layering

Spread the backing wrong side up and tape the edges down with masking tape. (If you are working on carpet you can use T-pins to secure the backing to the carpet.) Center the batting on top, smoothing out any folds. Place the quilt top right side up on top of the batting and backing, making sure it is centered.

Basting

Basting keeps the quilt "sandwich" layers from shifting while you are quilting.

If you plan to machine quilt, pin baste the quilt layers together with safety pins placed about 3″–4″ apart. Begin basting in the center and move toward the edges first in vertical, then horizontal, rows. Try not to pin directly on the intended quilting lines.

If you plan to hand quilt, baste the layers together with thread, using a long needle and light-colored thread. Knot one end of the thread. Using stitches approximately the length of the needle, begin in the center and move out toward the edges in vertical and horizontal rows, approximately 4″ apart. Add 2 diagonal rows of basting.

Quilting

Quilting, whether by hand or machine, enhances the pieced or appliquéd design of the quilt. You may choose to quilt-in-the-ditch, echo the pieced or appliqué motifs, use patterns from quilting design books and stencils, or do your own free-motion quilting. Remember to check your batting manufacturer's recommendations for how close the quilting lines must be.

Binding

Trim excess batting and backing from the quilt even with the edges of the quilt top.

DOUBLE-FOLD STRAIGHT-GRAIN BINDING

If you want a ¼″ finished binding, cut the binding strips 2¼″ wide and piece them together with diagonal seams to make a continuous binding strip. Trim the seam allowance to ¼″. Press the seams open.

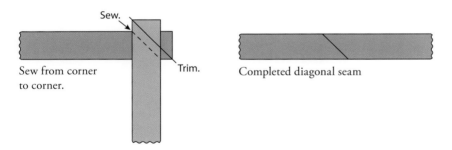

Sew.

Sew from corner to corner.

Trim.

Completed diagonal seam

Press the entire strip in half lengthwise with wrong sides together. With raw edges even, pin the binding to the front edge of the quilt a few inches away from a corner, and leave the first few inches of the binding unattached. Start sewing, using a ¼″ seam allowance.

Stop ¼″ away from the first corner (Fig. A), and backstitch one stitch. Lift the presser foot and needle. Rotate the quilt one-quarter turn. Fold the binding at a right angle so it extends straight above the quilt and the fold forms a 45° angle in the corner (Fig. B). Then bring the binding strip down even with the edge of the quilt (Fig. C). Begin sewing at the folded edge. Repeat in the same manner at all corners.

Continue stitching until you are back near the beginning of the binding strip. See Finishing the Binding Ends (next) for tips on finishing and hiding the raw edges of the ends of the binding.

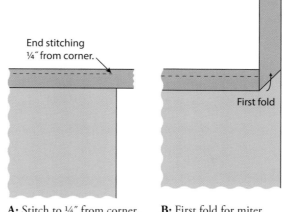

A: Stitch to ¼″ from corner.

B: First fold for miter

C: Second fold alignment

FINISHING THE BINDING ENDS

Method 1

After stitching around the quilt, fold under the beginning tail of the binding strip ¼″ so that the raw edge will be inside the binding after it is turned to the back of the quilt. Place the end tail of the binding strip over the beginning folded end. Continue to attach the binding and stitch slightly beyond the starting stitches. Trim the excess binding. Fold the binding over the raw edges to the quilt back and hand stitch, mitering the corners.

Method 2

Refer to ctpub.com > *scroll down to* Support: Quiltmaking Basics and Sewing Tips > Completing a Binding with an Invisible Seam.

Fold the ending tail of the binding back on itself where it meets the beginning binding tail. From the fold, measure and mark the cut width of your binding strip. Cut the ending binding tail to this measurement. For example, if your binding is cut 2¼″ wide, measure from the fold on the ending tail of the binding 2¼″ and cut the binding tail to this length.

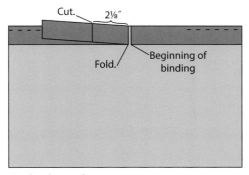

Cut binding tail.

Open both tails. Place one tail on top of the other tail at right angles, right sides together. Mark a diagonal line from corner to corner and stitch on the line. Check that you've done it correctly and that the binding fits the quilt; then trim the seam allowance to ¼″. Press open.

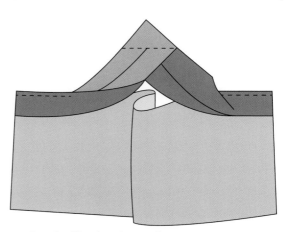

Stitch ends of binding diagonally.

Refold the binding and stitch this binding section in place on the quilt. Fold the binding over the raw edges to the quilt back and hand stitch.

Wedding Star

Grandmom with grandchildren

FINISHED QUILT: 20″ × 20″

Here is a bonus project for you to teach a younger child in your life some quilting artwork. Depending upon the age of the child, you will determine what the child is capable of doing. This was a one-day project made by my granddaughter, Brighton, age 8.

MATERIAL

Yardage is based on 42"-wide fabric; a fat quarter is 18" × 20"–22".

Bright colors: 5 fat quarters or ¼ yard of ombré print

Background (white or black): ¾ yard

Binding: ¼ yard

Backing: 21" × 21"

Batting: 21" × 21"

Double-sided fusible web: ¾ yard (My preference is Steam-A-Seam 2.)

Thread: Variegated thread for quilting

CUTTING

WOF is width of fabric.

Bright colors
- Cut 5 strips 4" × 12" total.

Background (white or black)
- Cut 1 square 21" × 21".

Binding
- Cut 1 strip 4" × 22".

Double-sided fusible web
- Cut 5 strips 4" × 12".
- Cut 1 strip 4" × 22" for binding.

Prepare the Diamonds

1. Follow the manufacturer's instructions for applying the double-sided fusible web to the wrong side of each of the bright 4" × 12" strips.

2. Before the paper is removed from the back of the fabric, have the child draw 1" parallel lines on the paper side.

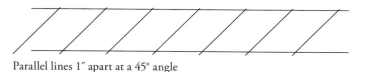

Parallel lines 1" apart at a 45° angle

3. Have the child cut out the diamonds with scissors.

Prepare the Background and Make the Star

1. Make a template from the Wedding Star E pattern (page 95). (Refer to Cutting from Templates, page 10, for more information about making and using templates.)

2. On the background square 21" × 21", find the center of the fabric by folding it into quarters. Use your template E to draw 8 diamonds on the fabric with a marking pencil to make an eight-pointed star.

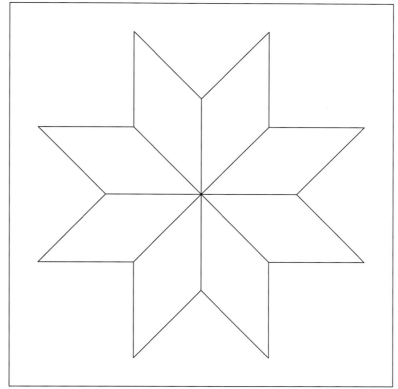

8 diamonds

3. Peel off the fusible web paper from the fabric diamonds and place 9 diamonds inside of each marked diamond.

> **TIP**
>
> Depending on the skill level of the child, it may be easier to place the diamonds inside of the larger diamond by drawing lines inside of the diamond. The diamonds do not need to be lined up perfectly; this creates a more modern and abstract quilt.

4. Press fabric diamonds into place following the fusible web manufacturer's directions.

Quilt and Trim

1. Draw lines 1″ apart from side to side across the quilt top.

2. Sandwich the 21″ × 21″ backing, 21″ × 21″ batting, and quilt top. Safety pin all layers together.

3. Using a walking foot on the machine, stitch on each 1″ line. After the complete quilt is stitched, go back and stitch between the 1″ lines. Then stitch one more time between these lines.

4. Trim the quilt to 20″ × 20″.

Attach the Binding

1. Apply the 4″ × 22″ strip of fusible web to the wrong side of the binding strip. Follow manufacturer's directions. Do not remove the second layer of paper backing yet.

2. Cut into 4 strips ¾″ × 22″. Finger-press in half lengthwise.

3. Remove the paper off the fabric strips and place the quilt edges in the folds. Press into position and

trim ends of binding off. Flip quilt and press binding on the back.

4. Topstitch 3 times on top of the binding about ⅛″ apart.

Brighton, age 8, at the sewing machine

Asher, age 7, cutting diamonds

Asher's *Wedding Star* quilt variation

PATTERNS

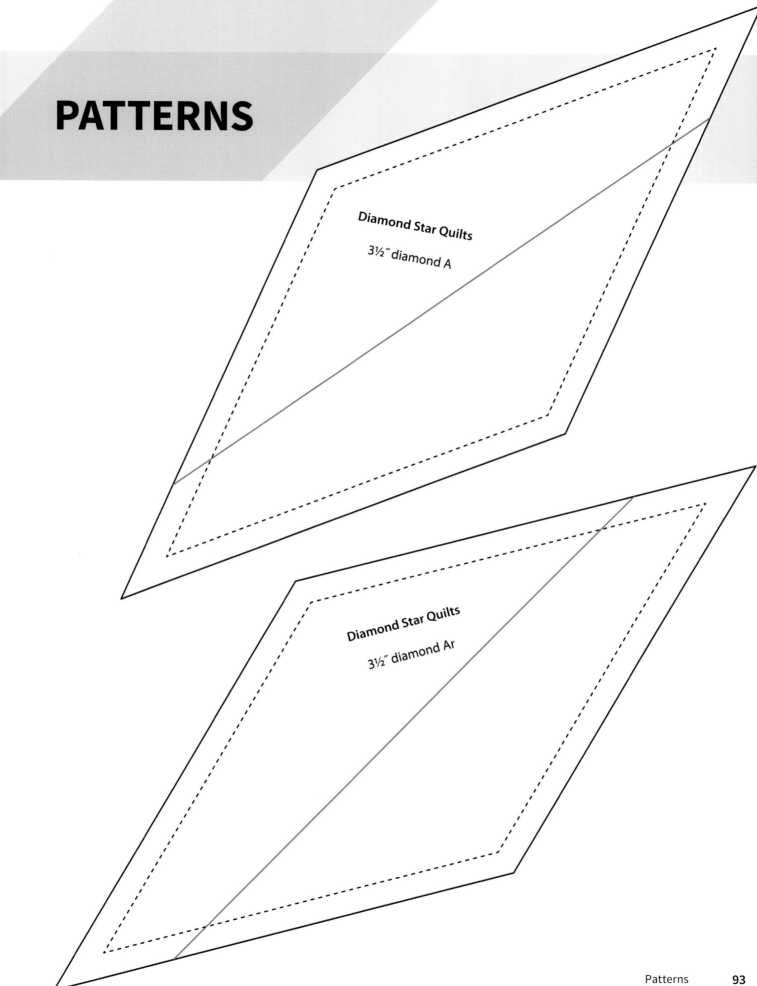

Diamond Star Quilts

3½″ diamond A

Diamond Star Quilts

3½″ diamond Ar

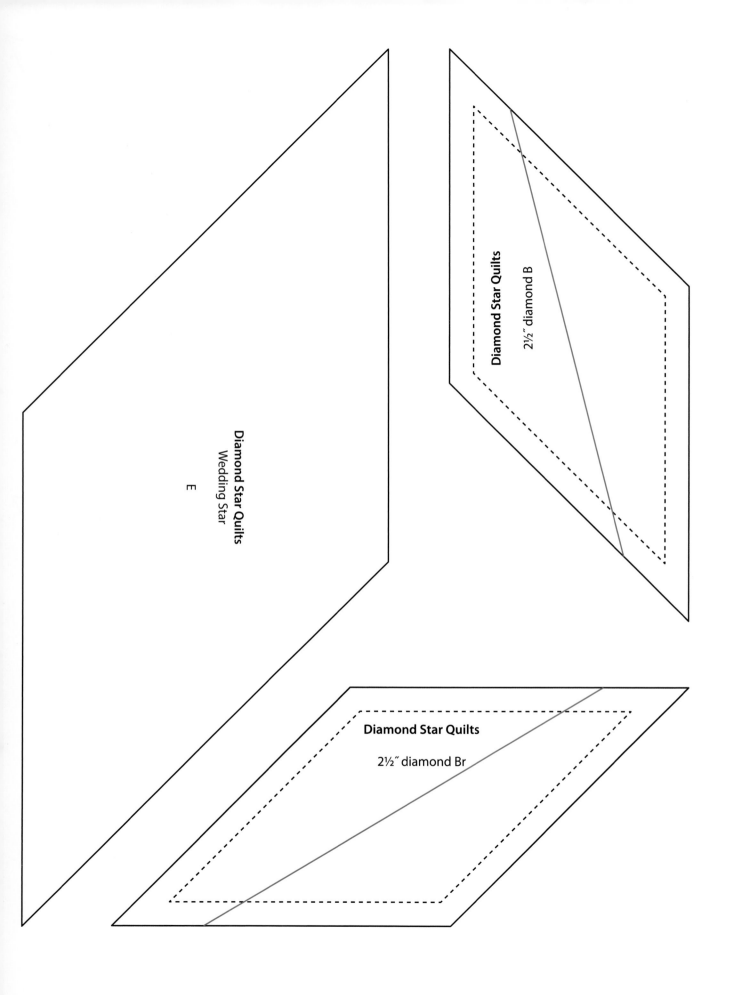

Diamond Star Quilts
Wedding Star

E

Diamond Star Quilts
2½″ diamond B

Diamond Star Quilts
2½″ diamond Br

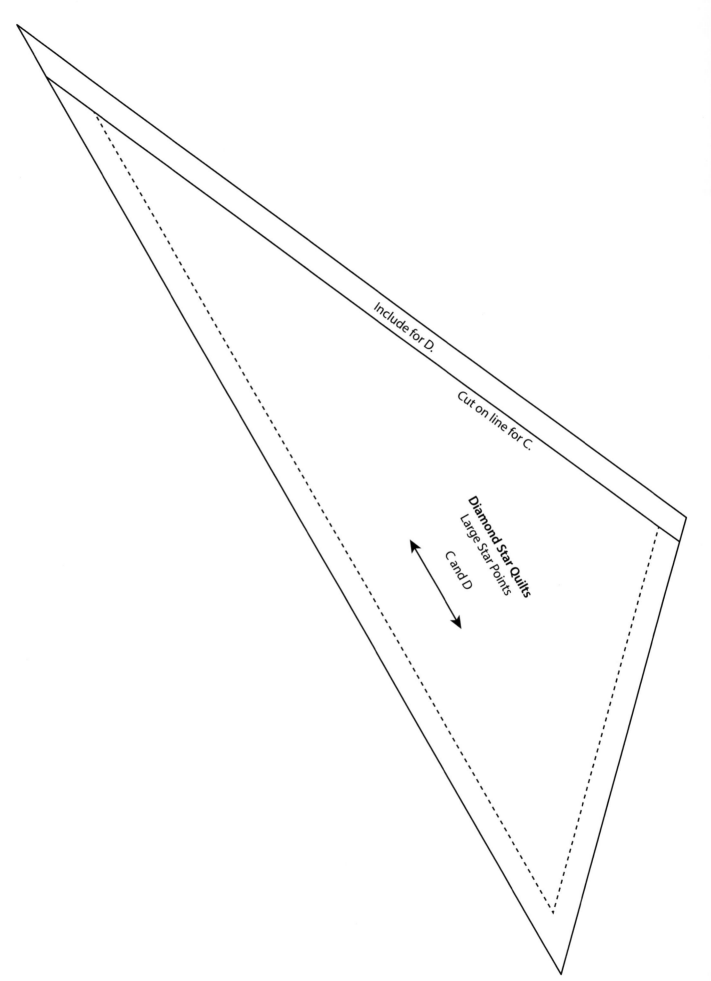

Include for D.

Cut on line for C.

Diamond Star Quilts
Large Star Points

C and D

ABOUT THE AUTHOR

Barbara H. Cline is a quilt designer, author, and teacher who loves to share her techniques with others. She started creating quilts in her teens. Barbara has more than 37 years of experience in quilting and teaching classes. This is her sixth book published by C&T Publishing.

Barbara currently teaches classes at local quilt shops and gives lectures, trunk shows, and classes nationally and internationally. Her latest travels have taken her to Dubai and Kuwait. She loves to design and piece quilts from her home in Shenandoah Valley, Virginia. The focus of her work is traditional quilts with a new spin. She loves the journey and seeing what she will create next; it is the mystery of planning the next quilt that keeps her passionate about designing and creating quilts.

She has enjoyed entering and placing in the Paducah quilt contest New Quilts from Old Favorites. Two of Barbara's quilts have won in different years: *Seven Sisters* and *Dresden Plate*. The Paducah Quilt Show, the Quilt Odyssey, the Mid-Atlantic Quilt Festival XVII, and the Hoffman Challenge have all displayed Barbara's wallhangings.

Barbara comes from a close-knit Mennonite family of quilters. Every year the women gather for a sewing retreat, where they quilt, sew, and follow other creative pursuits. The family members and their quilts were featured in the Virginia Quilt Museum's exhibition Five Generations of Mennonite Quilts. Barbara also has had her own exhibit at the Virginia Quilt Museum: *A Creative Quilting Odyssey by Barbara Cline*.

Visit Barbara online and follow on social media:

Website: delightfulpiecing.com

Pinterest: /quiltingal

Also by Barbara H. Cline:

Available as eBooks only

Available as eBooks and Print-On-Demand only